Table For Two

Edited by Christina Hamlett

Copyright © 2018 Christina Hamlett

All rights reserved.

ISBN-13:
978-1985134744

ISBN-10:
1985134748

Cover photograph and design by Christina Hamlett

In fond dedication to Aunt Liz and Uncle Bob.

In a lifetime of trekking the globe, it was never unusual for them to expand their table for two at restaurants to include servers, chefs and even total strangers seated nearby. Upon entering the dining room, Aunt Liz would often pause at a table to inquire about a particular dish that caught her eye and ask if it was something she should order. On the way out, she might notice someone was eating an entrée or dessert she herself had just enjoyed. "Weren't those raspberries just perfect?!" she'd say. Whenever time permitted for a longer conversation, it would likely lead to an exchange of addresses … and the start of many a new friendship.

My favorite Aunt Liz story, though, was after she became a widow and flew to Southern California for a visit with us. We ensconced her in a nearby hotel in Pasadena with the promise of returning first thing on Saturday morning to take her out for sightseeing. Upon our arrival, we discovered she wasn't in her room, nor did she carry a cell phone so we could call and find out where she was. (Seriously but it's bad form to lose one's aunt when she hasn't even been in town 24 hours.)

As we debated what to do, we noticed there was a wedding reception spilling out of one of the hotel's banquet rooms. And there, in the midst of all the celebrating, was Aunt Liz with a champagne flute and surrounded by a group of guests. The fact they were all laughing suggested she was regaling them with amusing stories. "What a coincidence that you met people you knew," I remarked. "Oh, I've never seen them before in my life," she replied in preface to regaling *us* with everything she had learned about the bride, the groom, the in-laws and even the caterers while she was waiting for us to come collect her.

And I'm sure no one in the wedding party ever questioned that she was someone's charming aunt and had every right to be there drinking bubbly and eating cake.

TABLE OF CONTENTS

ACKNOWLEDGEMENTS

INTRODUCTION (and Table For 1,500+)   3

DINNER WITH THE BUTTERFLY WHISPERER   7
By Sara Etgen-Baker

THIS ISN'T WHAT I ORDERED   11
By Sophie Ricci

UPTOWN GIRL   17
By Kevin Eldritch

A LESSON IN BIGOTRY   23
By Shayla S. Womack

TEA WITH BARBARA   29
By Anita G. Gorman

WOO-WOO WONTONS
   AND THE GREAT WALL OF CHICKEN   33
By Nancy McCulley

THERE'S NO MORE ROOM ON MY PLATE   37
By Liz Larson

DINING WITH THE GREAT PRESTO   41
By Lori Menken

NAKED LUNCH   47
By Patricia Bowen

A PAGE IN TIME   51
By Margaret Pascuzzo

FRIDAY RITUAL   55
By Janet Caplan

JUST LIKE IN THE MOVIES   59
By Lois Kiely

JUST DESSERTS   63
By Mary Langer Thompson

BUCKET LIST BISTRO By Lorelei Kay	67
TEA FOR TWO By Kate Guilford	71
THE LAST TIME I SAW PERRIS By Nina Ramos	75
SOULFUL BONDING By Sarah Stein	79
LUNCH IS INCLUDED By Raghavendra Rao	83
TABLE FOR ONE By L. J. Hecht	87
OUR CANADIAN SUNSET By Terri Elders	91
ABOUT THE EDITOR	95

ACKNOWLEDGMENTS

In appreciation of my hard-working judges—Katie, Donna, Jeremy, Leanna, Rory and Alyson—for choosing the best of the best essays that were submitted this season for consideration.
I couldn't do it without you!

INTRODUCTION
(and Table For 1,500+)

Memories are made around meals.
You may not remember what you ate,
but you remember everything else ... including the company you kept.

When I started reflecting on some of the dining experiences I've had between childhood and present-day, it was amazing the clarity with which I could recall who was across the table and yet very little about what was on my plate.

- Lunches at the Copper Coffee Pot during the summers I spent as a preschooler with my grandmother.
- The first time I went to a hotel restaurant by my teenage self in Orlando and a magician pulled the tablecloth right out from under my dinner without breaking a single dish or glass.
- A succession of bad dates in my 20s and 30s with men who were horrible tippers.
- The first candlelight dinner I cooked for the knight in shining armor who became my beloved husband.
- The first time I broke bread with the woman who has now been my best friend and soul sister for well over a decade.
- The in-room picnic for my birthday at a B&B in Mendocino that turned out to have a prophetic consequence on our lives and careers.
- My breakfast meeting with a werewolf—the culmination of a 50-year crush dating from the original *Dark Shadows*.
- The times we have solemnly raised our glasses in toasts to those no longer with us ... and the fond memories such rituals summon forth.

The fact that my husband and I are both gourmet chefs means that a lot of meals have graced our dining room table over the years. That we're as much into presentation as we are the food prep itself also means we are now on a moratorium insofar as buying more dishes, stemware, placemats, napkin rings and materials for seasonal centerpieces. Whether it's a celebratory occasion or just coffee and juice as we read the newspaper, neither one of us is shy about making every sit-down repast An Event that is both delicious and photogenic. Would you put every painting you owned in exactly the same picture frame? We feel the same way about setting the table.

It's not uncommon for us to have three-hour dinners at home, sometimes even longer if we're having guests. And what do we talk about during this time? For the most part, we usually can't remember, focusing only on how much we're laughing and having fun, grateful for every moment we have been given to spend together. Do we remember everything we ate and drank? To be honest, I've taken to posting mouth-watering pictures on Facebook, a practice which then prompts friends to ask for the recipes. My, my but what did we do prior to social media except to describe these meals in words, not photos? Yet magically—and every time—seeing any of those photos brings back the aromas, tastes and textures as vividly as when we first enjoyed them.

Travel—like culinary adventures—has likewise figured prominently in our lives ... and what's not to love about discovering new eateries and people-watching while on vacation? Even with the passage of years, we remember conversing in Spanish with the owner of a Cuban restaurant in the heart of Paris. The giggles of laughter from the full-bodied hostess in Adelaide, Australia who could easily have channeled Blood Mary and serenaded us with *Bali Hai*. Eavesdropping during a wine country lunch as a cougar dominatrix at the table next to us explained her relationship "rules" to her much younger male companion. The eclectic assemblage of evening diners at the Hanohano Room atop the Sheraton Waikiki, most notably a young Asian couple who never spoke a single word to each other during their entire meal and yet smoked one cigarette after another from the open carton on the table between them. Meeting our spunky Edinburgh solicitor, Fiona, at an Indian buffet we would never have discovered on our own. Ordering my husband's birthday dinner totally in German at a Viennese restaurant ... and being pleasantly surprised not to get a braised typewriter and a side of shoelaces. Having the wrong seafood entrée at Sam's in San Francisco delivered to me by a gruff, sixtysomething waiter who, when my husband pointed out the mistake, responded with an indifferent shrug and "So what? She'll like it."

For a lot of people, I think the association they have regarding dining with others not only comes from how old they are but also from the amount—or lack—of interaction they experienced at the family dinner table when they were growing up.

Was it a convivial communal table in which everyone excitedly talked about his/her day at school or work?

Was it a repressive environment in which children were strictly meant be seen and not heard ... and couldn't wait to escape?

Did swing-shifts and extracurricular activities mean that—with the exception of holidays—it was virtually impossible to get everyone together in the dining room at the same time?

Were holiday meals an anticipated wellspring of joy or a dreaded tableau of tension?

Have ingrained habits of grab-and-go cause people to literally lose their sense of taste?

And how did the emergence of TV trays in the 1960s segue to the 21st century acceptance of texting and emails and the idea that a meal could only be enjoyed if something entertaining was going on, something much more interesting than having to converse with anyone who was in the same room?

The diversity of essays received for this anthology competition don't just reflect the authors' relationship with food; they reflect expectations about the relationships they have with others. Whether it's the newness of dipping into the dating pool, meeting prospective in-laws, sharing a bittersweet reminiscence, bridging a cultural divide, seeing a different side of a family member, or simply enjoying the old-shoe comfort of a significant other, the judges had no easy task in choosing the 20 best of the best submissions for publication.

We hope you will enjoy them as much as we did.

Christina Hamlett, Editor

(and Table for 1,500+)

In April of 1912, R.M.S. Titanic set sail as the largest ocean liner ever built. To accommodate the appetites of more than 2,200 people on board, a staff of 80 worked 24/7 in the ship's trio of galleys to prepare approximately 6,000 meals a day.

A partial list of the larder manifest reveals:
2,000 barrels of flour
40,000 eggs
75,000 pounds of fresh meat
11,000 pounds of fresh fish
10,000 pounds of bacon, ham and sausage
40 tons of potatoes
800 bundles of fresh asparagus
1,500 gallons of milk
10,000 pounds of sugar
3,500 pounds of onions

1,750 quarts of ice cream
2,200 pounds of coffee
20,000 bottles of beer
1,500 bottles of wine plus 70 additional cases
Over 190 cases of liquor

While the first and second class passengers were accustomed to the concept of fine dining and multiple courses, even the passengers in steerage had no complaints about the White Star Line's daily fare which included hearty vegetable soups, fruit, roasted pork, fresh fish, steak and kidney pie, and plum pudding. In addition to having their meals presented on crisp linen tablecloths and being waited on by uniformed stewards, they were able to enjoy something they had never had back home: several days of complete leisure.

As an aficionado of all things Edwardian, I had decided to add to my husband's collection of cookbooks with a copy of *Last Dinner on the Titanic; Menus and Recipes from The Great Liner*. How on earth, we wondered, were some of the first class passengers able to waddle around on the decks after consuming a decadently rich nine-course dinner?!

To our delight, the recipes themselves had been scaled down for servings of 4-6. Therein, we saw a wonderful challenge: to select a handful of courses and recreate our own Titanic meal. That the 100th anniversary of the ship's sinking (April 14, 2012) fell on a Saturday was all the convincing we needed to turn our intimate table for two into a tribute dinner for the over 1,500 passengers and crew who never reached their destination.

After setting the stage with a CD of music from the era, we sat down at 5pm with Focaccia Crostini with caviar, chives, egg and Crème Fraiche. The beverage was Rose Champagne. Next came Potage Saint Germaine (a Spring pea soup) accompanied by Madeira.

By this time, we were playing the haunting soundtrack from *Titanic, The Musical*. For the main course, it was Filets in Red Wine Mushroom Sauce served over potato cakes. A Bordeaux wine was served.

We, of course, saved room for dessert: Chocolate Mousse Cake with Cognac.

The evening plan was to follow dinner with *Titanic's* star-crossed Kate and Leo. Although we had been cleaning up as we had been cooking, there were still a few items that required our attention before we could settle into the movie. As I stood at the dishwasher, my glance happened to fall on the nearest clock.

A shiver went down my spine with the mental-math realization that at the exact moment we were finishing our dinner, RMS Titanic had just struck the iceberg a hundred years previous.

DINNER WITH THE BUTTERFLY WHISPERER
By Sara Etgen-Baker

I entered Whispering Oaks where I found the large French doors of the day room flung wide open; the August air—light and fresh—gently blew the long, crisp, white curtains to and fro. I walked through the doors toward the verandah and saw Pop sitting outdoors amongst some zinnias surrounded by a rabble of butterflies.

He was slumped over in his wheelchair, his limp left arm tied to the chair's railing. He looked up and waved with his good hand. "Sara!" he called with delight. My breath caught in my throat, and I choked back the tears. I closed my eyes and felt the pull of my childhood memories urging me to leave.

You can't turn back; he needs to see you, reminded the voice inside my head.

But I can't bear seeing him like this. It's hard.

Yes, it's hard, but he needs to see you. So, you must be brave. Be brave for him. The voice answered, firm as a rock. *Don't turn back. Not now.*

I opened my eyes; a mixture of sunlight and shadow filtered through the large oak trees casting a warm honeyed tone along the narrow footpath in front of me.

Remember, continued the voice, *don't let him see you sad or upset. He needs your strength.* I swallowed hard; squared my shoulders; and meandered my way along the footpath toward Pop, my legs unsteady beneath me.

I sat down next to Pop and laid our lunch on the picnic table in front of him. "Da...da...dinner for ta...ta...two!" He flashed me an impish grin. "Re...re...remember?"

"Yes, Pop! I sure do!" I leaned toward him and gave him a kiss and big hug. "Summer afternoons, we'd sit together at the picnic table in our backyard, eating burgers and drinking chocolate milkshakes while we watched the butterflies dance around Mother's zinnias."

"Ya...ya...yes." He nibbled on his burger and sucked on the straw as best he could, taking short drinks of his chocolate milkshake. "Sooooo ga...ga...good!" La...la...love you!"

"Love you, too, Pop."

I squeezed his right hand and took a long drink of my own milkshake. Minutes passed by, and a little blue butterfly landed on my nose. Then a big yellow butterfly gently floated over and landed on Pop's shoulder. Soon a kaleidoscope of them floated up and down around him like a swirl of multicolored petals. I watched in awe and remembered when butterflies swarmed around him in our backyard; and, for most of my youth, I truly believed Pop possessed some type of magical ability that attracted butterflies. Later, though, I convinced myself he didn't necessarily possess magical butterfly powers believing instead that Pop simply made them feel welcome and safe. Regardless of the reason, the butterflies gravitated toward him like iron shavings to a magnet. And there was no denying it; he was then and was still *the butterfly whisperer.*

Time passed imperceptibly as we continued eating our burgers and watching the butterflies as they fluttered from flower to flower. Occasionally one of them landed on the stem of a flower that had already passed its peak, its petals blackened at the edges and curling. It folded its wings neatly upward and partook of the flower's nectar, seemingly unaware that summer would quickly become fall; that the leaves would soon tumble; and that the nights would close in, chilly and long. But the butterflies and flowers continued dancing together as one, living in the moment without a single thought about the future or the past.

I, on the other hand, drifted back to those summer days when I found myself in Pop's company. On one such day, Pop discovered me sitting at our picnic table crying over the fates of the butterflies in our backyard.

"They only live a few days," my lips quivered around the words.

"My darling daughter. Nothing lasts forever, but you needn't be sad for the butterflies; they live a beautiful life," he said in a comforting voice. "Remember, the butterfly counts not months but moments. So, it has enough time." He then went inside the house; made us chocolate milkshakes; and returned to the picnic table where we drank in silence relishing the butterflies that flittered around Mother's zinnias.

On another summer day, Pop drove me to a wooded area near our home for the sole purpose of capturing butterflies. "Once you spot a butterfly, approach it slowly so as not to startle it." He handed me a butterfly net, demonstrating how to sweep the net forward, flip it over the handle, and flatten the net bag so the butterfly's wings closed. "Now, using your other thumb and forefinger, reach into the net and grasp all four wings and remove the butterfly."

I followed his instructions, eventually netting a giant swallowtail butterfly. "Now, whisper a wish and let it go."

"Let it go? Seriously!? What's the point in capturing it in the first place?"

"Well, according to Indian folklore if you want a wish to come true, you must first capture a butterfly and whisper your wish to it. And since the butterfly makes no sound, it cannot tell your wish to anyone but the Great Spirit who hears and sees all. As thanks for giving the butterfly its freedom, the Great Spirit always grants the wish." Pop winked at me and smiled. "So, whisper your wish and let the butterfly go."

Pop squeezed my hand, jolting me back to the present. "La…la…love you."

I kissed him on the cheek. "Look, Pop!" I pretended to capture a butterfly between my thumb and forefinger. "I caught a butterfly!"

"Wh...Wh...Whisper." His eyes sparkled, vibrant as ever; but when he tried to wink, he couldn't. "Ma...ma...make wa...wa...wish," he said using disjointed words.

But watching Pop try to wink or talk was more than my heart could handle; so I closed my eyes and whispered, "Oh Great Spirit, erase the stroke and make my father whole again." But no amount of wishing would ever make my father whole again.

"I...I...had enough time," Pop clasped my hand. "Da...da...don't wo...wo...worry. I be free soon. Bu...bu...but I not a...a...afraid. I...I...ready to go." A single tear dropped from his eye. "Uh...uh...understand?"

"Yes, Pop." My chin trembled. "I understand." And although I understood, I just couldn't bear the thought of losing him. But like the butterflies I'd loved as a child, I knew he'd be gone soon—sooner than I wanted. "Oh, Pop," I gulped hard. "You have the grace and soul of a butterfly. I love you."

Throughout the remainder of summer, Pop and I continued watching butterflies outside the verandah. But I could not keep summer with us forever, nor could I halt the changing season. The flowers on the verandah withered; the leaves tumbled and rustled about; and the nights eventually closed in, chilly and long. And one-by-one the butterflies vacated the flowers on the verandah and began their annual migration southward. Pop, too, vacated the verandah and began his own migration of sorts. And in that moment of loss, my world collapsed; and my heart broke into a thousand pieces.

Years have come and gone since Pop's passing. Although the pain of losing him has diminished, I still miss Pop and sitting with him at our picnic table; sharing a milkshake on a warm summer afternoon; and watching the butterflies flitter around Mother's zinnias. But that picnic table now sits in my own backyard; and during the warm summer months, I frequent it indulging myself in a milkshake and watching the butterflies dance around the zinnias my husband planted. And although they don't gravitate toward me like they did Pop, a single butterfly occasionally lands next to me. I'd like to believe it's Pop sitting next to me, and we're once again eating burgers, drinking milkshakes, and sharing our father-daughter table for two.

Sara's love for words began when her mother read the dictionary to her every night. A teacher's unexpected whisper, "You've got writing talent," ignited her writing desire. Sara ignored that whisper and pursued a different career; eventually she re-discovered her inner writer and began writing memoirs and essays, many of which have been published in anthologies and magazines including Chicken Soup for the Soul, Guideposts, Times They Were A Changing, and The Santa Claus Project.

THIS ISN'T WHAT I ORDERED
By Sophie Ricci

My parents had what's called "a good divorce." My teachers, my friends' parents and even the school psychologist Mom briefly hired to help me cope—they all labeled it the same thing. *Good.* For me, how could something be "good" if two people who swore to be together forever woke up one day and decided it just wasn't working?

That was pretty much the chronology. The three of us went to a movie on Friday night and, over Saturday breakfast, they announced that they were divorcing. There wasn't any shouting, yelling, nasty blaming each other. There wasn't even a third party that caused one of them to stray. Looking back, it was such an ordinary, matter-of-fact Saturday breakfast that I remember checking the calendar to see if it was April Fool's Day. On Monday, though, Dad started putting his clothes and some boxes in the car and it hit me that my life would never again be the same.

He took an apartment a few blocks away so it would be easy for me to go back and forth. They had shared custody but Mom was the one I stayed with because it would make things feel more "normal." What's normal for an 11-year old? Who knew? I had friends at school whose parents had split and their lives were anything *but.*

Still, I soldiered on, *soldiered on* being a phrase I read in a book somewhere. They both came to my events at school and in sports and put forth all the appearance of still being happily married. So much so I began thinking this break from each other would cause them to realize what they were missing and they'd fall madly back in love again. And when they got re-married, I would be in the wedding party!

Some of the best times during this confusing period was my dress-up date at The Russian Tea Room with my dad. He'd pick me up and off we'd go to lunch or tea and dessert—usually once a quarter—and I learned everything I know about elegant table manners from watching other people. I was also impressed he knew the names of all the waiters and they would treat him—and me—like we were visiting royals. It was during these times we'd either be celebrating something like a birthday or he'd share a surprise.

There were three events, though, that are permanently frozen in my brain. The first is that my mom started dating someone just after I turned 13. Moms are not supposed to be dating *anyone*! Even worse, he had twin boys that were four and that their mother liked to dress in matching outfits head to toe. When they wore stripes and beanies, they looked like Tweedledum and Tweedledee. I told Mom in no uncertain terms that if—

horrors!—she married this man and I acquired them as little brothers, I was not, not, not going to babysit them. She assured me that she wasn't going to rush anything.

The second event was a few months later. Over my favorite dessert at The Russian Tea Room, Dad told me that he was considering taking a job in Australia. It was in his field of environmental conservation and he was pretty excited. While I was happy he'd be saving kangaroos and koalas and maybe even Tasmanian devils, did it mean I was never going to see him again? He told me he'd be back for symposiums and conferences and he'd make sure he had plenty of extra time built in for the two of us. "You could even come and visit me during school vacation," he said. "Would you like that?" I had told him about Mom and the icky twins and he suggested I'd probably *welcome* a chance to get away from them now and then in the event they became a permanent part of my life.

I wasn't sure how to process all this. Their *marriage* was supposed to be permanent. Our dress-up dates at The Russian Tea Room were supposed to be a permanent father/daughter routine. And I for sure would never, ever ask Mom's boyfriend to take me there because he wouldn't know how to act and he wouldn't know the names of any of the waiters.

The good thing is that Dad wouldn't be leaving until the end of the year because he had to finish out projects at the place he was working. Could I but hope the Aussies would get tired of waiting for him and retract the offer? The bad thing is that I knew it would all be weighing on my head up until when it for sure happened.

The third event happened in late October. Dad told me he had a surprise—which meant a dress-up date at our favorite place. I think Mom knew what it was but her lips were sealed about it. I, of course, was hoping the surprise was that he was staying in New York ... permanently. Now *that* would be worth celebrating!

So I put on my favorite dress and shoes and made sure my hair—which was long and straight—was perfect. He called Mom to ask if she could drop me off and he'd just meet me there. There was something sad in her eyes as I got out of the car. I didn't know if she was sad he was going to Australia or tears-of-joy-happy he had decided to stay here because of the two of us and they were going to get back together. Maybe him having her bring me was part of his plan—that she'd secretly valet the car and then they'd walk in hand-in-hand and shout "Surprise!"

My favorite waiter greets me with a deep bow. "Welcome, Miss Ricci. How very nice to see you."

He tells me the rest of my party hasn't arrived and would I care to be seated. When I see a table setting for three, I know my suspicions are accurate. Maybe the entire restaurant is in on the surprise and that makes me very happy.

TABLE FOR TWO

I spot my handsome dad as soon as he walks in. I also notice there's a young girl with him who has curly red hair and her arm in a cast. Maybe they just walked in together. Except he is gently leading her to *our* table.

"Siobhan," he says, "I'd like you to meet my daughter, Sophie. Sophie, this is Siobhan."

She smiles—I see she's wearing a mess of braces on her teeth—and says, "Jack has told me lots about you."

What???? Why is she calling my dad by his first name like she *knows* him? Why isn't she calling him Mr. Ricci like kids my age are supposed to do with teachers and other adults?

Dad is pulling out her chair. She's not *eating* with us, is she?

"I like your hair," she says. "Mine's too curly."

It's a compliment and Dad waits for me to acknowledge it.

"What happened to your arm?" I blurt out instead.

She says she broke it at her last soccer game.

"But her team still won," Dad proudly adds. "Right, kiddo?"

How and why would he know this unless—no, don't even *think* it—he was actually *there*?! And why is he calling her 'kiddo'?

Is it possible for blood to boil? Because that's what I think mine is doing.

"Uh—Earth to Soph ...?" I hear him say. Were they talking while I was scowling and fuming and I missed something?

She leans into him and says in a whisper I can easily hear, "I don't think she knows."

"Knows *what*???" I say in a voice that *everyone* can hear.

Dad gets an upset look on his face and rakes a hand through his hair. I think it's a universal gesture dads make when they don't know what to do. He looks at me with apology in his eyes. "Your mom didn't tell you?"

"Tell me what?"

"Siobhan's mom and I ... have been dating."

This is even worse than my mom dating the guy with Tweedledum and Tweedledee. I wonder how many *other* things that my parents aren't telling me.

"Since you girls are the same age and have a lot of the same interests—"

The only thing I can think to ask is if it's serious.

Siobhan gives a little cough and asks to be excused to the ladies room.

"Sure, honey. We'll wait to order til you get back." *Honey*?! How much worse can this get?

He turns back to me. "I know you probably have a lot of questions." In the next breath he says he's surprised Mom didn't tell me first. "Her own life's moving forward and I'm just as happy for *her*."

Well, I'm not happy for *either* of my parents because they both seem to have forgotten how *I'd* feel. He confesses he didn't want to confuse me prematurely with a parade of girlfriends.

So now there's been a *parade* of them?! When did he have time?

"Figure of speech," he explains. "Ana and I met at work but we thought it best to take it slow and not say anything until we knew how we truly felt about each other."

Does this mean Ana's kid was lied to, too? Maybe we *do* have lots in common …

"How *do* you feel?" I ask, not sure I want to hear the answer to this.

"Happy. Optimistic. Ready to take on the world."

I suddenly remember there's a bright spot in this. Dad's world is about to take him to Australia. It's far away from me but it's also far away from a girl who's *not* me and she and her mother will just have to get over it and steal someone else. Unless …

I ask him if they know he's moving to Australia.

Again, sad eyes and another hand-rake through his hair. "Ana and Siobhan are moving to Australia, too. Not right away but—"

The world has fallen out from under me.

He reiterates that this doesn't change anything about the two of us. He'll still be back for visits and I can come and visit him. Except the family-stealers will be there, too. He tells me after he takes Siobhan home, we'll have a long talk. A talk that's probably supposed to make things better except I know it won't.

"Maybe you should go see what's keeping Siobhan," he suggests. Not a suggestion really. A direct order.

I go downstairs to the ladies room. She's sitting on a settee and crying.

"Dad wants to know when you're coming back," I inform her. What does *she* have to cry about? *I'm* the one who's being deserted.

She looks up at me, swallows hard and says, "You're the lucky one, y' know."

"Huh?"

"You get to stay in New York and keep all your friends and teachers and everything familiar."

"So?"

"Australia's far away and we won't know anybody."

Yeah, except my dad. I ask her why she doesn't ask if she can stay behind with her *own* dad and live with *him*.

She audibly sniffles and tells me she doesn't have one.

I don't know why but that makes me feel sad for her. "Maybe my dad and your mom will break up," I remark. Maybe the two of us could hatch a plan to bring that about …

"My mom's happier now than before," she replies. "She deserves a happily ever after."

Maybe we *do* have lots in common. Annoying as the twins are, would I want my own mom to stop seeing someone *she* loved?

"We should get back upstairs," I tell her, "or Dad will send out a posse."

She grabs my hand. "I'm sorry, Sophie."

I tell her it's not her fault, that there's no accounting for what parents do to pull the rug out from under us. "We'll just have to work through it." I add the word "together" and she forces a smile.

And as we go upstairs, a new thought dawns. A world away, I'll have something I never had before. A sister.

In 2010, Sophie moved to Australia after almost four years of emails, Skype and visits with her step-sib. Both girls graduated with honors from University of Canberra and have developed their own line of fashion accessories. "We're not getting rich," Sophie says, "but we're having fun." This essay is her first foray into publishing. Siobhan is working on a business book for work-at-home moms. On Manhattan vacations, The Russian Tea Room remains their favorite place.

UPTOWN GIRL
By Kevin Eldritch

"Neh, he's just my dry-cleaning guy."

I don't mean to put myself down by that but I always wondered if that's what she said to her friends if they ever saw us together and asked her who I was.

Yes, I *was* her dry-cleaning guy who picked up her clothes and brought them back all freshly pressed and on wire hangers. My father always said there was no shame in a good day's work. My own good day's work included working for the dry cleaner's, waiting tables in Hell's Kitchen, doing acting gigs off-off-off-Broadway and going to school to get my business degree.

A world apart.

I was Billy Joel to my own Christie Brinkley. She was tall, slim, blond and tan. A true California girl even though she grew up someplace in New Jersey and the only view out her bedroom window was grimy smokestacks, not swaying palm trees.

I, on the other hand, *was* from California—a disclosure she found fascinating. I wish it had been someplace more alluring like Hollywood or Beverly Hills instead of Modesto but I like to think it counted as California all the same.

I noticed her right away. I don't know that she noticed me as much as she noticed the plastic-wrapped clothes I was carrying.

"Should I give you a tip or something?" she asked. She smiled at me and her teeth were white and perfect.

"No, that's okay. All part of the service."

Was there anything about this goddess that *wasn't* perfect? I was also smart enough to know she was way out of my league. There were probably scores of guys lined up to take her out and take her anywhere she wanted to go. I wasn't that guy.

A couple of months into my unrequited infatuation, I was doing my dinner shift at an Indian restaurant in Hell's Kitchen. Once upon a time Hell's Kitchen was the absolute worst place to be in all of Manhattan. Nowadays, there's a waiting list to get in if you're a prospective restaurateur. One of my fellow waiters was off sick and I was doing double-duty.

I walked up to one of his tables and there she was. I don't know why I felt myself go all red and embarrassed. I mean, seriously, she wouldn't recognize me from anyone, would she?

She was with some girlfriends and gave me a strange, sidelong look like you think you know someone but you're not quite sure from where.

"Oh, hi, she said flashing that beautiful smile.

"You *know* this guy?" one of her friends said.

"Of course," she proclaimed. "This is—"

"Kevin," I filled in the blank.

"Sorry," she said with a giggle. "Brain freeze. How nice to see you!"

"Likewise," I responded, still having no idea what *her* name was.

"Kevin's in my building," she said and her girlfriends all nodded approval. Not exactly a lie. I *was* in her building a lot. I just didn't *live* there.

The rest of the evening, I purposely hovered around the fringes of their conversation, desperately trying to pick up some clues about my uptown girl. By the time I brought dessert, the group had dwindled down to just her and one other person. So, too, had the tone gone from laughing to depressed, her friend frequently leaning in to squeeze her hands and tell her it would all be okay. I heard the name 'Bill' a couple times. Was Bill her boyfriend? Had he broken up with her? Was that why she was trying not to cry? What a jerk. I already hated him for upsetting her but a part of me saw a glimmer of hope that—oh, who am I kidding? A girl like her and a guy like me?

Her friend went to the ladies room. If my life were a movie, I slide into the chair next to her and ask if there was anything I could do. This, however, is real life and waiters aren't supposed to pretend they can just sit in a seat they're not worthy of. And so I stood there, smiled and asked if she'd like more tea. To my delight, she said yes. To my greater delight, her friend came back and said she had to get home. No, it still didn't give me permission to take her place but the restaurant was starting to thin out and my remaining customers didn't seem to need anything.

"You have the advantage of knowing my name," I said, "but I don't know yours."

Not exactly true. I knew her *last* name but only because it was on the dry-cleaning tags.

She extended her beautifully manicured hand. "It's Zoe."

*****

Have you met my girlfriend, Zoe?
This is my fiancée, Zoe.
Eldritch party. Table for two.
Hi, we're Kevin and Zoe—Ben's parents?

Come on, if you're going to invent conversations about a nonexistent girlfriend, what's wrong with inventing nonexistence offspring, too? The only problem with all this daydreaming is I had no idea when I'd see her again. Even if I did, who's to say she wouldn't be with 'Bill'? Just because I dropped off her dry-cleaning didn't mean I was going to go all stalkerish.

And then one Friday night I was at the restaurant and guess who walked in? Zoe. By herself. There to pick up a takeout order. She smiled when she saw me. (A good sign.) She told me she'd been stood up and didn't feel like cooking. I heard myself blurt out that there's a small table back by the kitchen if she'd like to eat her dinner there.

"Why would I do that?"

Projecting more confidence than I felt, I told her I could walk her home after my shift (which ends in half an hour). To my amazement, she told me that would be very sweet. She also apologized she couldn't remember my name but I'm okay with it. There'd be plenty of time to remind her on our walk (which is clear in the opposite direction of where *I* live).

I remarked that a guy would have to be a jerk to stand her up. She agreed with me but didn't volunteer anything further. "Do you like to jog in the park?" she asked out of the blue.

"Love it," I lied. The next thing I know, she's asking if I'd like to meet her for a run the next morning.

To me, running and talking don't really go together, and talking is what I'd really rather be doing. Still, it's a chance to be together. We high-fived each other at the door of her apartment building.

*****

I'm winded but trying not to look like a wuss. Could she not have told me *before* this that she ran track and field in high school and won medals for it?

"This isn't really your thing, is it?" she asks as we stop at a bench so she can do some stretching exercises.

I'm hyperventilating. "What gave me away?"

She laughs and asks me what kinds of things I do for fun. I tell her I like theater, old movies, cooking—

"Cooking? Seriously?"

"Started out as a necessity and then I discovered I love throwing stuff together."

"Hmmm ..." she replies.

I should pounce on the chance to ask her if she'd like me to cook for her sometime, but the window of opportunity slams shut on my fingers before I can get the words out.

"I hate to waste a run," she says. She's wistfully looking at the path as if it's calling to her and I am functionally dead weight.

"Maybe I could try it again next Saturday?" I offer.

People jog all the time. How hard can it be? If I run everywhere between now and next weekend instead of walking or taking the train ...

She's shaking her head. "My friends are throwing a birthday party for me so the day's kinda full."

"So your birthday's next Saturday?" Oh what an Einstein I am.

"Tuesday," she replies, "but Saturdays are better for a party."

Dare I hope for an invite? Probably not. Probably 'Bill' will be there. I ask her what her plans are for her *actual* natal day.

She shrugs. "Nothing yet. I was hoping—" She doesn't finish her sentence. "No biggie."

But I can see in her eyes she's seriously disappointed in someone who was supposed to make her birthday special.

"Listen, I know we don't really know each other but—" My brain is turbo-charging to make this come out right. "Maybe *I* could be your plan."

"You mean like dinner?"

"Wherever you'd like to go. Just name it."

She thinks for a moment and tells me there's a restaurant she's been to at the top of the building where she works and that it's really nice.

I know which one she means and it's also really pricey. That's not what bothers me, though. "Um—I was thinking maybe I could take you to someplace you haven't been with—" I bite back the name 'Bill' and substitute it for "anyone else."

"Like where?"

I know exactly where it'll be. "You like Italian food?"

She nods.

"Great. 'Cause there's this funky mom and pop trattoria in Brooklyn with the best spaghetti you'll ever taste!"

I even know what table I'll ask for. It's a cozy booth for two by the fireplace. Not that we'd need a fireplace this time of year when summer is holding on as long as it can.

She confesses she's never been to Brooklyn. I tell her we should make a whole day of it.

"But it's Tuesday. I have to work."

"Can't you call in sick?"

She arches a brow. "And nobody would think that was suspicious? Calling in sick the day of my birthday?"

I tell her it's only suspicious if you call in on a Monday or Friday because everyone thinks you're trying to make it a long weekend. "Didn't you ever play hooky from school?"

Of *course* she didn't. She probably also had perfect A's in every subject.

"I guess I could *think* about it," she muses.

"Okay but this is a limited time offer. I may have to ask someone else to spend the day with me."

But of course I *won't* because this is the only girl I have eyes for.

"I could call you Monday night and let you know," she suggests.

Except she doesn't have my number and I don't have hers and neither one of us has anything to write with. I scan the park and a short distance away I see two older ladies sitting on a bench. I tell Zoe I'll be bright back. I tell the ladies I'm sorry to bother them but does either of them have a pen and a scrap of paper.

While one of them looks in her purse, the other looks past me and sees Zoe. She smiles, probably having figured out I need the paper for a phone number. "Good luck, young man," she calls after me.

Zoe tucks my number into the zippered pocket of her yoga pants.

The path is calling her and I watch her jog off, her ponytail swinging.

Okay, it wasn't exactly like I extracted a promise. Maybe she *won't* call but at least she has my number.

I gingerly retrace my steps back through Central Park, pretty sure I've torn a ligament but not really caring.

The first thing I do when I get home is to grab a pen off the kitchen counter and draw a squiggly heart around next Tuesday's date.

September 11th.

After graduation, Kevin decided to use his business degree and go into the restaurant business with two of his best buds. They facetiously put their names on a waiting list for a coveted spot at Hell's Kitchen but expect they'll be in their 90s by the time anything ever materializes. Meanwhile, Kevin enjoys a happy home life with his beautiful wife and their 12 year old son. Her name is Zoe. His name is Ben.

A LESSON IN BIGOTRY
By Shayla S. Womack

"Are you sure you don't want to just stay in tonight and watch one more episode?" I asked as I sat on the edge of the bed in protest. He was frantically rushing around the room, putting things in his pockets.

"Of course not! My parents have been waiting forever to meet you."

I sighed and fell back onto the bed. New people have never been my strong suit. Don't get me wrong, I'm a delight once you get to know me, but I tend to be a bit awkward upon first introductions. I'd never had a boyfriend before much less had to meet his parents for this first time. I had been dreading it since he told me they were coming into town just a week prior.

"It'll be fine. I promise. They'll be on their best behavior." He leaned down and kissed me on my forehead. "Promise."

We walked into the restaurant, one he said his mother insisted on coming to. "Nothing but the best for my Jakey and his new lady friend", he'd said mocking her. My eyes widened as I looked up at the breathtaking crystal chandelier above our heads.

Jake gave his last name to the greeter who escorted us past the front desk, through the crowded tables, up some stairs and behind a velvet curtain. I saw them first; they were just as he'd described. Mr. Carmichael was big around the middle. He had laughing lines around his mouth that may have given his true nature away had it not been for the sternness of the rest of his face. Mrs. Carmichael was softer yet she looked as if she only made facial expressions on special occasions for fear of wrinkles. I suppose this night would've constituted as one of those occasions.

They saw us but didn't realize I was looking at them as well. A look of concern was plastered across their faces and if I wasn't mistaken a bit of anger as well. As we walked closer, Jake's father's face turned a bright red. He tried to get up from the table but his wife hushed him and ushered him to sit down. As confused as I was, Jake seemed not to notice. Maybe Mr. C just had gas.

"Mom! Dad!" Jake said as he embraced his parents. His mother met his squeeze with full force while his father held back, more reserved. "I'm so happy to see you guys! This is my girlfriend, Lucky," he said, beaming at me.

"Oh Lucky, kind of like a dog's name? Lucky, short for anything?" his mother said. They had both sat down by now which led me to believe that a hug for me was out of the question.

"No, it's not short for anything. My dad just said when he saw me, he felt like the luckiest man in the world. So ... Lucky," I said, smiling.

"Oh your father? How wonderful that you have one, dear." Her thick Southern accent nearly choked me.

Mr. Carmichael continued to shake his head in disbelief. It was clear that he was uncomfortable. I was sure the gas was getting to him and his stomach couldn't take it much longer.

"You ok over there, Pops?" Jake asked half-jokingly. His father offered nothing. The waiter walked over and saved us all.

"Hello everyone. My name is Juno´t and I will be your server tonight. Can I start anyone off with some wine? We have an excellent selection tonight."

Mrs. Carmichael, Jake and I each went around telling Juno´t our preferred beverages. Mr. Carmichael sat there.

"What did he say he wants to know, Judy? I can't understand a word he's saying."

"Just give him your drink order, honey. Don't be difficult," she said, smiling over at us.

"I'm just sayin' if he spoke a little English, it'd be easier for me to understand what he wants" Mr. Carmichael mumbled. That's when it hit me, this is the "gas". "Yeah I'll just take a Coke, light ice."

Juno´t walked away, leaving me alone with nothing to fill the air but my awkwardness and Mr. C's "gas".

"Mr. Carmichael, Jake tells me you're the CEO of a marketing company back in Alabama. I actually --" He got up, throwing his napkin on the table.

"Judy, where are those bathrooms?" She pointed to a hallway and away he went.

"Dad!" Jake said calling after him, but Mr. C was already out of sight. "I'm sorry, Luck, I don't know what's gotten into him."

Jake looked genuinely upset at not knowing what was wrong with his dad. I wanted so much to tell him, to ease the confusion from his face but there was a small part of me that was mad at him for not already knowing.

"Oh it's fine, don't worry about it." I said. He squeezed my hand underneath the table.

"Lucky, dear I'm so sorry I keep staring, but your hair. It's so ethnic lookin'." She reached out as if to touch the mop of manicured curls and coils atop my head. I knew in my heart that if she touched them I'd have to swat her hand away, she'd hate me for sure and Jake would have to break up with me.

"Mama, stop it!" Jake said, shocked and embarrassed. Thankfully she retreated her hand.

"What, Jakey? I'm just trying to get a sense of a little culture like you're always telling me." I smiled politely and picked up my menu, giving it a fake once-over.

After moments of awkwardness, Mr. C finally made his way back to the table. However, instead of sitting he plucked his coat off of the chair and through it over his shoulder. "Come on, Judy; we're leaving."

"Alan..." Judy said.

"No, I've had enough", he said looking at her before turning his eyes towards me. He squinted them in disgust as if he were trying to figure out a particularly hard math problem. "I don't know what the two of you are getting at but enough is enough".

"Mom, Dad, what's going on?" Jake looked genuinely hurt.

"Alan, just sit down for a second. Jake honey, your father and I are just confused. We don't understand what kind of stunt you're trying to pull. Is she pregnant, honey?"

"Excuse me?!" Jake and I said in unison. "Of course she's not," Jake continued.

"Oh thank God," Judy said fanning her face. "Lucky, I'm sure you are a nice girl but you and my son, it's just not ... not right."

"Mom!" Jake said cutting her off. "Lucky is my girlfriend. I brought her here to meet you both because she's important to me. I want her to be a part of my life for a long--"

"Jacob, that is enough," she said, returning the favor of being cut off. "I don't want to hear that kind of talk. Look what you're doing to your father."

We looked over. Mr. C had his fist clenched. I thought he was going to pop a blood vessel. Mrs. C reached over and rubbed his back. I looked over at Jake, pleading with him to say something, anything. He lowered his head and looked away.

I adjusted myself in my seat and bit my tongue, I knew I had to choose my next words carefully.

"I guess I shouldn't be surprised." I removed the napkin from my lap and tossed it on the table. "Mrs. Carmichael, I don't want to assume anything here so why don't you go ahead and explain what you mean by "not right"."

Surprisingly, she didn't look uncomfortable. She looked me dead in my eyes and said "Lucky. Let me see how I can explain this to you. We come from different worlds and honestly, you don't belong in ours. Lucky, there's no way Mr. Carmichael and I are going to be ok with you being in our family." She paused for a moment before leaning in to whisper, "And dear, imagine if the two of you had children. Little mixed babies running around the compound."

"Mrs. Carmichael," I said, closing my eyes and raising my hands in defense before clasping them back together. "I cannot think of anything I'd want less in this world than to become a part of this family."

"Lucky ..." Jake piped up.

"No. You don't get to speak up now. Do you hear yourselves? You don't want me to date your son because of the color of my skin? I've never met such racists--"

"Whoa!" Mr. and Mrs. C said in unison.

"Now you wait a minute. We are not...*racists*." Judy said as she looked around, smoothing out the front of her dress. "We love the Blacks and the Latinos. We have several of them in our employ. As a matter of fact, Jakey's nanny was a Black. She was with us for several years."

I looked over to Jake who had his eyes closed and his head hung. Shame and embarrassment washed over him.

"I don't even know why you're explaining anything to her." Mr. C said scoffing.

"Lucky, *racists,* is a strong term. You're blowing this a bit out of proportions. We just have certain expectations for the natural and just plain right progression of our family. I truly am sorry. You understand, don't you, sweetheart?"

I believe this was her version of sympathy.

"Mrs. Carmichael, Mr. Carmichael, how dare you sit there and say that I'm am not right or natural."

"We didn't say--"

I raised my hand to my lips, shhing her. "It's my turn now Mrs. Carmichael." She held her mouth open, shocked, but realized it was best if she went ahead and closed it. "For my whole life, my parents' life, my grandparents' life, for most black people, your "natural" order has never worked for us. The box you put us in doesn't fit. We've never been "right". But, we go along, try our absolute best to play by your rules knowing that no matter what we do, your rules, your tricks, your ploys, will never work in our favor. I've lived in neighborhoods you drive an hour out of the way to avoid but are now desperate to gentrify so that you can feel comfortable. I've worked jobs that you wouldn't even consider in your worst nightmares just to make barely enough to feed my families from day to day. I've gone to schools so overpopulated and so underfunded that it's a miracle anyone finishes. A miracle Mr. and Mrs. Carmichael; I am a miracle! I have to be twice as good to get half of what you have but that's still not enough is it? Is it?!"

The table is silent and all eyes are on me. "Of course not. I feel sorry for you, Mrs. Carmichael, for all of you. I really do."

I scooted my chair back and picked up my purse. Jake scooted his back as well. "No, Jake, you stay," I told him. "Your silence has been louder than anything anyone here has said." I put my coat on and walked away; through the velvet curtains and down the stairs. The crystal chandelier shook as I closed the door behind me.

All names have been changed for privacy reasons

Shayla Womack is a Cleveland, Ohio native. She received her undergraduate degree from The Ohio University and has recently moved to Savannah, Georgia to pursue her Masters degree in Dramatic Writing from SCAD. Shayla has always been a lover of words. She actively pursues any and all opportunities to share her thoughts/experiences in the hopes they may have an impact on someone just as her favorite writers have had an impact on her.

TEA WITH BARBARA
By Anita G. Gorman

At some point each of us remembers when we first became aware of our existence, the first event that we can actually remember and that seems to us the beginning of our lives, even though it isn't. For me it was a subway ride from my home in Elmhurst, Queens to the Swedish Hospital of Brooklyn and the subsequent elimination of my diseased tonsils and adenoids. I was, I think, only three when this terrifying event happened and I still remember, decades later, my fear of the hospital, conveyed to me, no doubt, by my worried parents, especially my mother, herself a bona fide graduate of the Swedish Hospital School of Nursing. I think she knew how many things could go wrong.

My terror increased before I succumbed to the ether mask and remained as I recuperated, lying in what was for all intents and purposes a baby's crib. The only respite from my fear happened when I was given ice cream, cold ice cream to soothe the burning in my little throat.

My imaginary playmates Johnny and Barbara accompanied me to the hospital. Going on the subway with Johnny and Barbara was often an adventure, since they would sit in seats near me, but not in my seat, since there was not enough room for the three of us. Sometimes unknowing passengers would sit right on the seats that Johnny and Barbara had been occupying, and then my little friends would have to quickly jump up and find another seat or hang onto one of those subway poles to keep their balance.

Johnny and Barbara were not imaginary to me; they were, in fact, more real to me than the people walking up and down 55th Road in front of our house or the looming presence of Public School 102 at the top of our street. I was a solitary little girl without siblings and without playmates when Johnny and Barbara came to live with us. They were very real to me, though my mother thought they were imaginary. What my father thought about this--if anything--I do not know.

An old woman named Mrs. Brimley rented a room in our house for a while. Now, decades later, I wonder who she was and where she came from and why she rented the back bedroom on the second floor before she was evicted by my brother's birth. An old woman with white hair who wore black dresses and sensible shoes, Mrs. Brimley became another person I could talk to in my loneliness.

I would often climb the stairs to the second floor of our home and visit Mrs. Brimley. I liked her, and she was a good listener. I had only one living grandparent, but he was in Sweden and I was in New York, so we never met. Mrs. Brimley was a kind of grandmother to me, at least for a short time, and she would always listen when I told her what Johnny and Barbara were doing and what sort of trouble their grandfather had gotten into.

The grandfather was always getting into trouble, and looking back now I can only imagine what he did. Perhaps he stole a cookie from my mother's stash of newly-baked Christmas delights. Maybe he spilled a glass of milk on the kitchen floor or let the water in the bathroom sink overflow onto the floor. Whatever my childish imagination could conjure up, Johnny and Barbara's grandfather did. I do not believe he committed murder. That was not something I could imagine. But he did go to jail, and Mrs. Brimley would nod sympathetically when I related the grandfather's latest mishap.

And so the days went by. I was happy to have Johnny and Barbara with me, and it never occurred to my parents to take me to a psychiatrist. Nor did Mrs. Brimley seem to think that my little friends' presence was cause for alarm.

The fog of memory makes it difficult for me to remember all the details of my tea parties with Barbara. Johnny usually didn't want to partake of "girls' stuff" and so he would often absent himself if Barbara and I wanted to play with dolls or take out my tea set and have a snack.

My tea set—now long gone—was blue and white and had what I would later recall as a Chinese design. I wasn't allowed to drink tea, and besides, Swedes preferred coffee, which I also was not allowed to drink in those early days. World War II was raging--it began the year of my birth--and the Thompson boys (I never knew their first names) from across the street were in the Army. So was Clifford Olson, who lived next door. Joe and Jack Hinchey, whose house was on the other side of us, were both in the Navy. It was quiet on our street, made more quiet, probably, by their absence and the worries of the parents and siblings of the soldiers and sailors, now so very far away, in Europe or in the South Pacific.

And so I would fill the teacups with water, and I would take a cookie or two from the pantry; I knew where my mother kept or hid things. And then I could carry on a conversation with Barbara while we had our tea party.

While Barbara and I chatted, Johnny would spend his time in the area between our garage and the Olson garage. It was the only place where grass grew, but it wasn't the kind of grass that people like to have in their front lawns. It was, I suppose, what we call crabgrass, interspersed with various weeds, and there was a tree, a birch tree, whose branches could be used to beat me if I were naughty. This was, so far as I could tell, an old Swedish custom. I do not remember being beaten with a switch of birch branches, but I was frequently threatened with the possibility.

While Johnny busied himself near the birch tree and the crabgrass between the two garages, Barbara and I would have a lovely conversation.

"Have a cookie, Barbara."

"Thank you, Anita."
"How is your grandfather?"
"He has been very bad."
"What did he do?"
"He ate the whole pie that my grandmother baked. Nobody else could have any."
"Is he in jail?"
"Oh yes."
"Barbara, I have a secret."
"I love secrets. What is it?"
"I'm going to have a baby sister."
"Really? I would like a baby sister. A brother isn't so much fun."

My mother had told me about the arrival of a baby sister. It would happen when summer was over, in September. I would be four and a half. I was excited.

Barbara spoke again. "If you have a baby sister, maybe you won't want to play with me."

"I will. I don't think babies do much, at least not when they first show up."

As it turned out, my aunt, whom I called Moster Malin, came to get me in September, just before my mother would give birth. We took the train from Grand Central Station up the east bank of the Hudson River to Peekskill, rode the De Matteis bus to Lake Peekskill, and then walked a good distance to Moster Malin's house. Uncle Otto, my dear uncle who died when I was seven, would be there to greet us and to love us.

But when I began talking about my baby sister, my aunt would caution me. "You know, Anita, you could have a baby brother."

"No, Mommy said I would have a baby sister," I insisted.

And then September 15th arrived and my father called to announce the birth of my brother David. Moster Malin, the phone in her hand, turned to me and said, "You have a little brother."

I shouted back, "You stinker!" The birth of my brother was obviously Moster Malin's fault. She was the only one who had predicted the possibility of the birth of a boy.

It was still warm enough to have a tea party in the backyard after I came back from Lake Peekskill and little David was ensconced in the bedroom formerly occupied by Mrs. Brimley.

"What happened to the little sister?" Barbara asked.
"She's a boy."
"Is that OK?"
"I guess so. Meanwhile, you are my sister."

Barbara smiled at me, and I finished my cookie and my water. After that, my imaginary friends, who had been so real, began to seem less present as the house filled with the sounds of a baby's cries. Johnny and Barbara disappeared forever soon after, when a new family moved into the house two doors away. Their daughter Irene, who was a year older than I was, took my imaginary friends' place. But life with Irene was not as pleasant and carefree as life with Johnny and Barbara had been. Now it seemed as though World War II had finally reached 55th Road. And there were no more tea parties with Barbara.

Anita G. Gorman grew up in Queens and is aging in Ohio. Her scholarly work has appeared in various publications. Her essay "Where Are You, O High-School Friends?" was published in Unfinished Chapters (2015) and "Finding Bill" in Finding Mr. Right (2016). Her short stories have appeared in Gilbert, Down in the Dirt, Dual Coast, Jitter Press, Red Fez, Speculative Grammarian, and Knee-Jerk. Her play, Astrid; Or, My Swedish Mama, will be produced in 2018.

WOO-WOO WONTONS AND THE GREAT WALL OF CHICKEN
By Nancy McCulley

"Mom's just getting old. She needs to feel like she's still in control."

I love my husband, Danny, to the moon and back but he has three older brothers that have been married longer than us and their wives all swear Mona has been a micro-manager for as long as they've known her. It doesn't matter whether it's about child-rearing, housekeeping, what we're wearing or how we've styled our hair, she barges right in with a barrage of unsolicited criticism and it's almost always hurtful.

Thanksgiving Dinner, though, is the worst imaginable.

She insists that it has to be held at her house every single year. We concede on this because all of our other relatives have dibs on Christmas. She gives everyone a detailed list of what to bring … and then delivers a litany of everything they did wrong.

Danny and his brothers have tried, unsuccessfully, to encourage her to dial it back on denigrating everyone's efforts so vocally at the dinner table. She insists that we're overly sensitive and need to get over it. As early as three weeks before, my sisters-in-law and I start getting migraines and upset stomachs just dreading what we'll be called on the carpet for doing—or *not* doing.

"Can't we just sit it out a year?" I asked Danny.

While Danny shares my sentiments and is sympathetic to all the stress his mother creates for the rest of us, he wasn't sure that boycotting Turkey Day was the best solution. "If we're not there," he said, "you know she'll talk about us the entire evening."

Personally, I'd rather be talked *about* than talked *at* and ruthlessly belittled for my specialty yam dish that has been pleasing my *own* side of the family for years. I proposed an alternative—that he talk to each of his sibs and their wives and we all make a pact to literally take a stand if Mona starts in on any one of us.

"But if we walk out," says one of the siblings, "where will we go?"

Danny is confident that it won't come to that. That Mona will be so thrown for a loop to be put on notice, she'll apologize and not make a peep the rest of the meal.

Wishful thinking.

We really try to ignore the little digs that she makes as we all start arriving. No sooner have we sat down and said grace, though, she launches her first nasty insult … at me.

Danny scoots back his chair, stand up and clears his throat. "This is supposed to be a day when we give thanks for being together," he begins. "Why must you always turn it into something ugly and hurtful when there's absolutely no reason for it?"

Mona goes on the defensive. I look around the table, hoping that everyone will stick to the plan we rehearsed. To my dismay—and anger—they're all looking down, suddenly fixated on their plates. Mona asks Danny why he's still standing up.

'Because if you don't apologize to each and every one of us, I'm afraid we have no choice but to walk out of this house."

I stand up next to him, interlocking my fingers with his.

Mona snorts at this and waves her hand dismissively.

I wait for the sibs and their wives to scoot back their chairs in solidarity. But they don't. They're that scared of her.

It's a moment of truth.

Even as we step out into the hall to put on our coats, no one joins us or begs us to come back.

Ever the guy who makes me laugh, Danny remarks as we're backing out of the driveway, "Well, it seemed like a good plan on paper …"

The question now, of course, is what we're going to do about dinner. It's too late to go home and defrost something. Danny also points out that we're too dressed up not to take advantage of having a date. I remind him that it's Thanksgiving and every restaurant in town has probably been booked for months by happy families that all get along with one another and don't resort to food fights.

Ever the optimist, he suggests we could try a couple of places in the hopes that maybe there were some last-minute cancellations.

Six restaurants later—did I mention Danny has the patience of Job?—we're starting to think a Thanksgiving dinner of any kind is never going to happen. We're also getting very hungry.

And then Danny spies something promising. It's a hole-in-the-wall Chinese restaurant with a neon sign in the window that says OPEN. There's only one car in the parking lot but Danny takes it as a sign of human life. A set of dangling bells jingle on the door as we step inside. Behind the counter, an Asian man of indeterminate years looks up from his newspaper and bottle of beer.

"Can you take two without a reservation?" Danny quips.

The man tells us we can have any seat in the house and we decide to take the window.

A moment later he comes up with two large, laminated menus.

Danny tells him we feel lucky to have found a place that was still open.

The man nods and takes our order for two beers.

When he returns, it's to tell us that he recommends the Woo-Woo Wontons and the Great Wall of Chicken.

"Are those your house specialties?" I ask.

In complete deadpan, he informs us that it's what he has left back in the kitchen and that he's done cooking for the night.

Danny grins. "Then that's exactly what we'll have."

He takes our menus and goes back to the kitchen.

"If we hadn't come in," I guiltily whisper to Danny, "he was probably getting ready to lock up and go home."

"Or maybe," Danny counters, "he has a dragon of a mother-in-law and he'd rather stay here and enjoy the peace and quiet."

It's a natural segue to the prior events of this Thanksgiving. Or, as it will later come to be known as The Event.

"How long do you think she'll stay mad at us?" I ask.

Danny is completely realistic when he predicts it will probably be Forever. Mona is The Queen of Grudges. Although we'd been married for 14 years, he suddenly began to relate stories I hadn't heard before. Stories about a lifetime of emotional abuse Mona heaped on her sons as well as her husband.

"You'd think she'd be happy we were all over-achievers and turned out successful," he said. "We were all trying so hard to please her, maybe even to 'earn' her love, that we didn't realize we were getting nothing but belittling, back-stabbing and ulcers in return." Was it any wonder she extended her potent vitriol to the brides who began joining the family fold. None of us were good enough, pretty enough or smart enough in Mona's opinion to 'steal' her sons away from her.

As we enjoy our very generous portions of Woo-Woo Wontons and that Great Wall of Chicken, we take turns speculating what happened after our departure from Mona's table. Danny is again accurate in predicting that no one followed our lead. "What do we do *next* year?" I ask.

My husband grins. "Maybe we should put in our reservation early for *this* place," he suggests. "It's pretty jumpin'." We also observe that the portions are big enough that we can ask for a doggie bag and enjoy our leftovers the next day.

Across the room, the proprietor has long since finished his newspaper and is immersed in a weather-beaten paperback Louis L'Amour.

"Are you okay?" I ask Danny. He's one of the kindest and most sensitive men I've ever known, and it had to have been hard to take what could well be the first step in a permanent rift and estrangement from the woman who raised him.

"It's funny," he replies, "but I'm actually feeling a sense of resolve and peace. Does that sound weird?" He wants to stay close to his brothers and his sisters-in-law but he expresses relief that he finally spoke his mind instead of continuing to enable and excuse his mother's nasty behavior. He has no expectation of being a model that the rest of them will follow and he's okay with it. Maybe sometimes, he says, bitterness and manipulation are so deeply ingrained that nothing can ever change it. He has no idea why she's the way she is since, as far as he remembers, his grandparents weren't like that at all. "I guess you either grow up emulating the people you love or you do a 180 and become the exact opposite."

The proprietor has come up to our table with a small plastic tray containing our bill and two fortune cookies. "No rush," he says. Which more times than not translates to *I'll expect to see cash or a credit card by the time I come back here.*

It's only then we realize we have been sitting and talking for nearly two hours. We also notice that outside the window, the first snowflakes of winter have started to fall.

Danny opens his cookie and reads, "'A change of scenery will restore your spirit.'"

He smiles at me and squeezes my hand. "I don't know. I think the view I'm looking at right now is restoring my spirit just fine." All these years later, this darling man still makes me melt.

I open mine and read, "'You will have a loving partner for life.'"

A habit of mine since fourth grade, I write the date on the back of each one and put them into my coin purse. I always like to see if these little strips of paper will prove prophetic.

Danny opines that he likes whoever typed these up.

We shovel the fragrant leftovers and white rice into cartons and put them in the flimsy white and red plastic bags that are the norm for Chinese restaurants. It will be a nice lunch for us while everyone else is hitting the malls on Black Friday and shopping with a vengeance.

As we step out the door and wish the proprietor a Happy Thanksgiving, we get only a wave of his hand. That Louis L'Amour paperback really has his attention.

Danny pulls me into his arms and asks me if I've had a good Turkey Day ... even without turkey.

Without missing a beat, I tell him it was perfect because I was reminded of what I am the most thankful for.

"Me, too, babe. Me, too."

The summer following The Event, Danny McCulley (a chemical engineer) was offered a dream job in Costa Rica. Nancy was more than happy to transport her home-based bookkeeping business, their two cats, and a houseful of furniture to a lively community of American ex-pats in Alajuela—new friends that love good wine, conversation, movies ... and Nancy's signature yams.

THERE'S NO MORE ROOM ON MY PLATE
By Liz Larson

It was a forgettable meal as far as the food was concerned. It could have been a burger, a salad, or one of the restaurant's all-day breakfasts served to those who crave eggs and bacon any time of day. We may have shared the fries that one of us ordered, but the other decided to nibble on after they arrived at the table. There was, most definitely, a Diet Coke on the table as that was, and still is, my drink of choice.

It was the ordinary, everyday lunch of a couple that was in love and thinking of a future together. Sitting at the table and enjoying the conversation more than the meal, we held hands and discussed our upcoming college classes, our plans for the weekend, and our love of the Bee Gees. We then began discussing our future and that's when the meal, and the day, took a very different turn.

We had met the previous year shortly after the start of college. I noticed this handsome guy behind me one day after a class we shared and asked him if he'd like to get a soda together. We went to the commons area and spent hours talking and laughing, and we knew right away that this was something special. I learned, quite some time after we started dating, that he was smitten with me from the first moment he saw me in class, and had not quite worked up the courage to ask me out before I had asked him. From that afternoon onward, we spent most of our time together outside of school and work, and the weekends were cherished time where we could take a day trip or go out on a date.

One night, we sat up until the wee hours of the morning dissecting the song, "American Pie" by Don McLean, infusing meaning into every phrase of the eight and a half minute song. This, of course, meant that we had to stay up even longer just to finish our schoolwork, but it was worth it to be together. Our time together was always exciting and enjoyed to the fullest. During our courtship, we took a ferry trip to Canada, we skipped through the tulip fields in the spring, we sang along to mutually loved songs, and occasionally stayed up all night just talking. We shared many meals together enjoying both the company and the food, from fast-food to our local "nice" restaurant for a big night out.

At times in the progression of our relationship, the occasional mention of the future and growing old together would come up. Of course, with this mention, the topic of children would bubble to the surface. We had differing thoughts and desires on becoming parents and, for a while, we each brushed those differences aside, even pooh-poohing the other's notions or insisting that, "You'll change your mind when we get married."

Eventually, though, the real-life discussion about this topic would need to happen as there was a great chasm separating our preferences—with him wanting many children and me adamant about having none. Oh, we could put off the inevitable for a period of time and just enjoy life, but sooner or later, this important talk would need to happen and the decision would need to be faced, and it was faced during that otherwise forgettable meal.

Our lunch that fateful day began to go unnoticed as our discussion intensified. We stopped nibbling on those fries or salad and started focusing on each other—really listening and understanding the dreams of the other person. What did we want from life outside of this circle of two? What would we each give, or give up, to be with this special person? Holding hands, we continued to share, to listen, and to truly understand.

I knew from the time I was a young girl, around the age of 12, and I boldly informed my mother that I was not going to have children. I knew this as unquestionably as I knew I would call my best friend after dinner or that my sister and I would get matching outfits for Christmas. My friends and family thought I would eventually change my mind as I was only 12 for goodness sake. Most certainly, by the time I was in my 20s or 30s, I would hear the ticking of the maternal clock. As it happened, by the age of 20, I was more certain of my choice, and by 30, after having been a birthing coach for friends, I knew, without a doubt, that my choice was right for me. I love children, but becoming a mother was not a life goal—it was not a need or a want in my life. It was, simply, my choice to not have children.

This wonderful man so wanted to spend his life with me and have children together and watch them grow up and send them out into the world. He wanted nothing more than to share the gift of life and love, and make the sacrifice of giving of yourself to your children. However, for either of us to give up our choice, our decision, or our life's calling for someone else's dream was something neither of us was willing to do. We both knew from the time we were children ourselves what we wanted in this world and what we wanted to give back to this world. He wanted to have a partner and children, where he could dedicate his life to caring for them, volunteering at their school, donating to their projects, teaching them, nurturing them, and exploring the world with them. Mine was a life dedicated to caring for others, volunteering for causes, donating to charities, learning new things, growing myself, and exploring the world meeting new people. You see, there would be no more room on my plate for children.

In William Shakespeare's *Hamlet*, Polonius wisely stated, "This above all: to thine own self be true," and when confronted with choices, we must search within ourselves and stand true to our inner authenticity. The two of us realized during our meal that neither of us should have to compromise on such a huge life-altering decision and with many tears shed, made the decision to go our own ways and make our lives without each other. We were both, above all, true to our own selves, and we knew what we were giving up to realize that truth.

The remainder of our meal was now room temperature—even the Diet Coke. Food untouched and ice melted, we sat in sorrow and silence. Though wretched and a bit broken, there was comfort in sitting together and being there for each other. There was also the knowledge that once we got up from the table and left the restaurant, we would never see each other again, never hold each other again. How long could we make our final meal last? How long could we sit at this restaurant before they kicked us out? I've been through broken relationships before and since, but this seemed more difficult because we still loved and we still cared for each other.

I heard from him many years later and he married a lovely lady, and they had their children together. They shared the miracle of birth, the terrible twos, the growing pains, puberty, and all the wonderful experiences of watching children grow up together. They shared love, goals, and dreams together because they both wanted the same things in life. He also shared with me that he knew he would be giving up something that day at lunch—the person that could take his breath away—but he wouldn't trade his life for anything in the world because he has the love and joy of his family. Choosing to be true to himself, he has made a wonderful life

During that lunch so many years ago, the food may have been forgettable, but the meal will long remain in our memories. We bared our souls, our dreams, and our hearts. With food that was left forgotten and uneaten, along with the sadness and tears piled on, there was no more room on my plate.

Liz thoroughly enjoys her life in Colorado with her wonderful husband, Dave, and their darling dog and two tuxedo cats. Her day job supports her love of learning, writing, and painting. She is an avid student of life and revels in new experiences.

DINING WITH THE GREAT PRESTO
By Lori Menken

My friend Sheri had just become an accredited psychic and decided to throw a party for herself to celebrate. "You have to come," she insisted. "I want to introduce you to the guy who painted my aura."

Apparently aura-painting is something he did for a living. Apparently Sheri thought the two of us could be soulmates. Not sure if she had an inside psychic track on this or just wishful thinking but I was curious.

His "gift," as she explained it, was to close his eyes, concentrate very hard, and "let the colors come"—the result being a garish swash of light and shadow, plus or minus a few zig-zags, which were meant to depict the subject's inner self, Zodiac sign, and universal worth.

"But how do you *know* your aura is marigold with a splash of magenta?" I asked when she showed me the finished product. (Heaven forbid one should be cursed with an unflattering aural palette and have to keep it in a hall closet.)

"Because his muse tells him so."

It was a cold, foggy Saturday afternoon. An hour and a half into the party, The Artist Formerly Known as Milton had yet to arrive.

"I can't imagine what happened to him," Sheri remarked, though consciously opting *not* to use her newly acquired degree and telepathic powers on such show-boating tricks as discerning where one's guests are.

The words were no sooner past her lips when—Voila! (or, rather, Presto!), the missing celebrity made his entrance, replete with short ponytail, John Lennon tinted glasses, and a midnight blue wool cape which he effortlessly shrugged off his broad shoulders to be caught by the person standing nearest the front door.

Who's the kook in the cape? I thought, finding it hard to get past his quirky wardrobe or the ponytail that looked like a wind-up key at the back of his head.

Having doffed his outer apparel with great panache, he was now making his way across the living room to where I had parked myself by the hearth. "You must be Lori!" he exclaimed as he reached for my hand. "I'd know your aura anywhere."

"And you must be Milton," I said.

Did I detect a cringe of embarrassment?

"Please," he insisted, "call me 'Presto'."

I resisted the urge to ask if that was 'Presto-with-one-exclamation-point-or-two?'

"Sheri tells me you're an artist," I said, even though his moniker seemed better suited to billing as a magician at a kids' party.

Almost immediately, he corrected me and said it was pronounced "artiste."

"What a dynamic milieu," I responded, figuring anyone who called himself an artiste would feel right at home chatting about his milieu as well.

"I am The Painter of Glow."

"'The Painter of Glow'," I thoughtfully repeated. "Is that sort of like Thomas Kinkade being 'The Painter of Light'?"

Apparently it's a faux pas of enormous consequence to make such brazen comparisons, no matter how clever they sound at the time. Presto was instantly ruffled.

"Kinkade is just an artist," he retorted. "He only paints what he *sees*. I paint energies that are *invisible*."

"If they're invisible, how do you know if you've got them right?" A legitimate question, I think.

"Because my muse tells me so," he replied.

"What does your muse say about *me*?" I asked, figuring that so many people are always asking me how to write a song that I should be able to turn around and sponge up my *own* share of free advice.

He lifted his wire-frame glasses off the bridge of his patrician nose and began squinting intently at my forehead. "I've never seen anything like this," he revealed, taking my hand and pressing my fingers to his lips. "My muse says it would take me an entire lifetime to capture the full spectrum of your inner radiance and spirit …"

Presto or his muse, I mused, must charge hourly.

"You," he declared, "are The Quintessential Goddess."

This guy was one smooth-talkin' idiot.

Sheri picked that moment to come bouncing up with a refill of wine. "How are we all getting along?"

"Did you know I'm The Quintessential Goddess?"

"No, I didn't," she replied. "Did you know Presto is The Painter of Glow?"

"Yes," I said, "I think we've established that."

LATER, THAT SAME DAY

"Have you had dinner yet?" he asked.

We hadn't progressed any farther than Sheri's hearth ever since his arrival two hours before, owing to Presto's fascination with telling me his life history. The rest of the guests—averse to venturing out into what had become a dark and stormy night—had broken into small herdlets and were liberally partaking of Sheri's more expensive bottles of wine.

"I know a wonderful little Italian restaurant," he continued. "Do you like minestrone? This place has the best minestrone in the city."

Hmm. Cold night. Hot soup. A free meal, albeit with an artist(e) whose ego would have put the State of Maine in shadow. I was also driving my own car which gave me the freedom to end the evening on my own clock. "Sure. Why not?"

The restaurant was located in what had once been an upscale shopping complex. Unlike the mega-malls which eventually lured away the bulk of its regular customers, it was still a collection of one-story Spanish-style buildings linked by open-air paseos and punctuated with sidewalk cafes that offered everything from Jewish Deli to Tandoori.

From the enthusiastic reception he received from everyone when we arrived, I could draw one of two conclusions: (1) He was more famous than I thought or (2) he worked there and this happened to be his night off.

Whatever the case, his wool cape was dutifully caught by one of the staff before it hit the floor and we were escorted to what would be the first of four tables before finally settling on the one which he felt put me (or was it him?) in the best light.

"Did I tell you about their minestrone?" he reiterated after ordering a pot of chamomile tea.

Although there were several items on the menu I might have been hungry for, my memory was tugged back to an earlier age and a book which—in its time—was the quintessential manual for teenage girls: *The Seventeen Book of Etiquette and Entertaining.* (1963 by Enid A. Haupt)

In addition to broaching delicate dining topics as "How can I find the ladies' room?" and "What should I do when he pays the check?" the book boldly addressed the issue of "the young man's finances."

I quote:

"If you order the most expensive thing on the menu, you may weaken your date's wallet; with the least expensive, you'll surely weaken his pride."

(This is the same definitive source which also extolled the virtues of coming-out parties, adding gloves to your ensemble for a "brisk, smart flourish," and declining any invitations to smoke during a job interview because "it looks too casual.")

Since he had already volunteered so many endorsements about the minestrone, I naturally assumed that perhaps the aura-painting business occasionally strapped him for dinner funds and minestrone was the best he could manage if he was paying for two.

"The lady will have the minestrone," he told the waiter.

"Will that be a cup or a bowl?" the waiter asked.

"A cup will be just fine," I lied.

Instead of ordering the same for himself, my companion proceeded to ask what all the specials were.

The list was lengthy.

"I can't decide between the Abbacchio Brodettatto or the Bistecca alla Fiorentina," he lamented.

"The Bistecca is especially nice, sir."

"That might be too heavy. How's your Cuscineti di Vitello?"

"An excellent choice."

"What about a salad? Does it come with a salad?"

The waiter replied they had an amusing Insalata di Funghi Crudi.

Presto scowled. "Raw mushrooms," he muttered in unabashed disdain. "I have some unresolved issues with them …"

I couldn't imagine what kind of 'issues' a grown man might have with mushrooms. I also wasn't sure why a quintessential goddess such as myself had become invisible as my date yakked amicably about whether he should throw in an appetizer of Anguilla Marinata, Caponata or stick with the house Bagna Cauda. I caught myself thinking the Beach Boys could have fun substituting some of the entrees for the lyrics that begin, "Off the Florida Keys, there's a place called...."

None of this exchange included an invitation for me to expand on my own order. I was tempted to pipe up I'd like a glass—nay, an entire bottle—of their priciest wine to wash down my minestrone.

"I'm feeling so positive about finally connecting," Presto said after our waiter had departed. "In fact, I'm feeling the need to share my latest vision with you. Would you mind?"

"Sure, whatever," I replied, suspecting he was probably going to share it with me whether I asked him to or not.

He reached for a cocktail napkin and asked if I had a pen. It was no sooner in his hand than he began to vigorously sketch what looked like a bunch of big rocks in a circle. "This is going to be my greatest creation. When the leaders of the world powers see it, they're going to lay down their arms and weep …"

A pretty heady prediction, I thought, especially since what he was drawing looked a lot like Stonehenge and which (I'm pretty sure of this) a lot of people on the planet, world leaders included, are already familiar with.

A few dramatic details later and he was finished, turning the napkin around for me to see.

"It looks like Stonehenge," I said. This was probably as much a faux pas as my earlier gaff comparing him to Kinkade.

"It's much *bigger* than Stonehenge," he said, impatient with my naiveté. "It's a message from Him."

"Him?"

With expression unchanging, he confided that God Himself had called him at home and commissioned him to sculpt this grouping of granite and take it on tour.

This raises some intriguing questions.
- What kind of long-distance service does He have?
- What sort of advance and/or royalties are involved when the Almighty commissions mortals to do something?
- How does one transport that much weight on a road-show?
- Will He make an appearance at the various gallery openings or just watch from afar?

"So does this happen to you often?" I asked. "Getting calls from God?"

Presto shook his head. "I was as surprised as you are, even though my muse hinted He was very pleased with my work and that I might be getting a call." In the next breath, he said he was also expecting a call from Oprah.

Between you and me, I've always given wide berth to people who profess to be Martians, witches, or time-travelers. After all, I once supervised a woman who told me she was from another galaxy and was just killing time as a typist until the mother ship came back for her. Hey, if her story was true, would I really want to alienate a bunch of, well, *aliens* in the event they were planning a conquest of Earth?

I decided to be open-minded about Presto's revelation God was telling him to go sculpt rocks—a task which, I might add, sounded much easier than the one He dumped on Noah.

"So what exactly are these rocks supposed to say?" I asked.

He earnestly proceeded to explain that each of them represented man's foibles: gluttony, greed, pride--

"Excuse me, but aren't those the same as--"

"Yes," he said, "but now He wants them depicted in stone." He smiled. "And this is the part where *you* come in."

No, I thought, this is the part where I go *out*. Unfortunately, my minestrone arrived and I was committed to at least another 20 minutes of inane conversation.

"Sheri tells me you write songs."

"Uh-huh ..."

"Picture this, then. Between my sculpture and your tunes, what would we have?"

"A rock musical?"

Behind those wire-frames, his eyes grew moist with tears. "You've read my mind."

Lyricist/composer Lori Menken teaches music theory, coaches her daughters' soccer teams, and is married to a fellow teacher so refreshingly normal and well-grounded that she wakes up every morning feeling blessed. She is also working on her first musical, which has absolutely nothing to do with Stonehenge, The Seven Deadly Sins or minestrone.

NAKED LUNCH
By Patricia Bowen

I'd been through a long, nasty divorce that upended my children's lives and left my emotions in tatters. Marriage had left a hurt in my heart, and I was reluctant to try again. But, after a few years, I met a man who helped me put the pain in perspective, in the past, where it belonged.

Grant was everything my ex wasn't and I was attracted to his calm inner sense of self, trusting it would envelope me and help me find my own peace. Slowly, it did. He taught me to make time for myself, to care about what my needs were, along with everyone else's.

It was brave of him to marry me, he childless, me with four young sons, two cats, four gerbils, a full-time job and little energy for anything else, except him. He was bright, interesting, adventurous, and I followed his lead, especially on the latter, keen to break my domestic routine whenever a rare opportunity arose.

And here it was. The boys were spending the day, the first day of summer, with their dad, and Grant and I were free to do grownup things. He was a gourmet cook and we both enjoyed teaching my children to experiment in the kitchen. But this meal was going to be for us, just us, a picnic.

"Leave it to me," he said, as soon as they were out the door. "You just kick back and let me spoil you."

So I stood back and watched as he sliced and measured and wrapped, savoring the anticipation of food and fun. He baked chicken in wine and then diced it into bite sized pieces, cut up grapes and apples and melon, made tiny sandwiches rolled up and sliced thin, and found two dusty bottles of Pouilly-Fume in the basement. No picnic basket, so we retrieved the wicker tub we used to haul laundry up and down the stairs, lined it with a blue and white checkered table cloth, and packed it with our portable feast.

In keeping with my kicking back, Grant was in charge of the picnic site, too. I assumed he'd find a place with tables and benches and walking trails, grass to lie down on while we watched the clouds go by. But no. He drove into an abandoned camp road that dead-ended at the edge of some dense woods and parked. The birds were chirping as they perched above us, and cicadas droned in the oaks. I could hear water spilling over some rocks nearby. I didn't know where I was, and I didn't care. I was alone in Eden with the man I loved.

We each took one handle of the repurposed laundry basket and made our way into the woods, frequently having to walk one in front of the other to squeeze between the trees.

"How much farther?" I queried.

"Until no one can find us," he replied.

"Why is that?"

"Because we're going to play a little game. Just you and me, love."

I went along, curious. We walked at least a half mile or so until we found a clearing, just large enough to spread out our tablecloth and then some, and laid out our feast. As he uncorked the wine I asked, "So, what's this game we're going to play?"

"It's called 'naked lunch'. Ever played it?"

"I've read the book. Or I tried to read it. It was a real downer and I couldn't finish it. But no, I've never heard of the game."

"Well, here's how it goes. You pick something you'd like to eat and I'll feed you a tidbit of it. Then, in exchange, I select an article I'd like you to remove from your body, maybe your watch or a shoe. Then we change places. I pick a food, you select something you want me to take off. We keep going until we run out of clothes or food, whichever happens first. Sound like fun?"

My body felt flushed, maybe from the wine, maybe from the explanation of the game. I looked around at the trees and dense brush, pretty sure no one would stumble upon our little party. If they did, we'd hear them coming. I was game.

We started with the sandwiches, one slice at a time, then alternated with pieces of fruit and chicken. I shyly took off an earring, he a belt, me a belt, he a shoe, and so on, until we were left with nothing more to remove and still some food and a whole bottle of wine. I lay on my back next to Grant on one side of the tablecloth, Eve to his Adam. The sun was warm on my skin, in places that weren't used to outdoor exposure. It felt good. Then I heard a crunch in the brush and, too relaxed to care who or what had made the sound, turned to see a young doe eying me warily. She stepped closer as I held out my hand. She sniffed it, raised her head and sniffed the air, then turned and ambled away. She didn't find us very interesting.

Of course we laughed. Of course we made love. Of course it started to rain.

By the time we threw our clothes on and got back to his VW Beetle we were drenched, as were the remains of our picnic. We sat in the cramped car and drank the other bottle of wine; it was warm, and it still had a vaguely smoky aftertaste. It put us both to sleep, wet duds and all, until we were awakened by a uniformed officer rapping hard on my window. "You folks all right in there? Hey. Everything okay?"

I roused and immediately touched my body, ensuring my clothes were properly on. They were, and still damp. I cranked down the window and smiled. "Yeah, officer. We just got caught in the rain and thought we'd finish our picnic here, in the car. We must have dozed off. Is it okay to park here?"

"Sure thing. But there's a curfew. You have to be out of here before sunset. Today being first day of summer, longest day of the year, bought you some extra time. Be safe now. Glad everything's all right."

When the officer drove out of sight, we giggled like naughty children. It wasn't too close a call, but close enough. I wondered what he would've thought, what he would have done, had he come upon us earlier in the day.

We got back home an hour before the kids, with just enough time to shower, unpack, throw our clothes in the wash, and put on a pot of coffee. I felt aglow, for just a few minutes, until my four raucous boys piled in the door, all talking at once about their day. They'd played mini golf, had lunch at the diner, went to see *Close Encounters of the Third Kind* on a wide screen and it was awesome. On the way home their dad got stopped for speeding, but the cop felt sorry for him with all those kids in the car and he let him go with a warning. "It was awesome, Mom. The whole day was awesome." No one asked what I'd done, but I'd had an awesome day, too.

That was almost 40 years ago. That marriage didn't last either, but every detail of the picnic memory did. I never played the game with anyone else. I never wanted to. I wouldn't be able to replicate the very first time I'd had a perfect feast.

Patricia Bowen writes novellas and short stories, mostly about women with complicated lives. She's been a copywriter, business owner, international coach and marketing manager, among other things. She lives in rural Georgia with her two cats whose job it is to keep the other critters outdoors. She's a certified master gardener and she writes gardening articles for her local newspaper and grants to support local libraries. Her website, still a work in progress, is www.PatriciaBowen.com.

A PAGE IN TIME
By Margaret Pascuzzo

"Come, dear," called James from the garden. "Come, we'll be late for our dinner reservation."

"I'll be right there," I answered from the bedroom.

I stole one last glance at myself in the full-length mirror as I prepared to join him. I had chosen my "little green dress" to celebrate my milestone birthday. It was one of James' favourite outfits, too, and one he often chose if I asked him what I should wear. The bright green of the dress brought out the auburn highlights in my hair. Donna, my hairdresser, had gone that extra mile and I came out of the beauty parlour looking 10 years younger than my 76 years. Matching shoes completed the look. Stunning, I thought!

I made my way to the front door, confident that I would blend right in with the ambiance of the Hotel du Vin, a high-end restaurant in Glasgow's fashionable West End.

"You look utterly smashing, dear!" exclaimed my date as he blew me a kiss from the porch.

"I love you," I said as I took what I thought was a well-deserved bow.

"One Devonshire Gardens," said James upon entering the taxi.

"Special occasion?" inquired the driver.

"Yes," we answered in unison.

"It's Margaret's birthday," James added.

"Congratulations!" The driver nodded as he slipped away from the curb.

We travelled through Glasgow's chic West End. On our way we passed a myriad of pubs, clubs and quirky shops whose main purpose was to cater to the body of international students who had chosen to study at the acclaimed University of Glasgow.

In a matter of minutes, we arrived at our destination, a sophisticated building nestled in a tree-lined avenue. My heart sang as I soaked up the neighbourhood. The street was a wealth of extravagant Victorian buildings in red and blond sandstone each adorned with artistic flourishes. Both James and I are products of Glasgow's West End and it's at times like this that we bask in the richness of our heritage.

As we entered the foyer, we were in awe of the colourful stained glass windows and the impressive wooden staircase which led to world class rooms and suites.

Almost immediately a maître de ushered us into the bar. As soon as we were comfortably seated, a waiter handed us a food menu and took our order for bar drinks. We perused the menu as we sipped our cocktails. It offered so many mouth-watering choices that we found it difficult to make a selection. We had to choose from an array of starters and main courses each inspired by French flavours. In the end, James selected vegetable soup, rack of lamb, pomme frites and a side of asparagus in sauce. I settled for roasted tiger prawns, rack of lamb, roast wedges and chantenay carrots.

To accompany our meal, James chose a bottle of French champagne. Our orders were placed and we were informed that we would be called to our table prior to our meal being served. We relaxed in the splendour of the bar. Subdued lighting complimented the oak-paneled walls. Tables, chairs and booths were of the highest quality. The room was packed with warmth and character.

"Let's have a toast," James suggested as he raised his glass. "Happy birthday!" he whispered.

"May all my birthdays be as happy as this one." I beamed.

Our eyes met and for one fleeting moment we were transported to a romantic world known only to us.

We were brought back to reality by the voice of the maître de.

"Excuse me Sir, Madam. Your table is ready."

We followed him into the main dining room and were seated at an intimate table for two. The room was exquisite. Soft lighting from a heavy drop chandelier enhanced the rich oak-paneled walls, the dark tables and leather chairs. Heavy curtains partially covered the bull's eye windows and a matching wall-to-wall rug completed the elegant décor. An open fireplace glowed on the far wall creating a welcoming atmosphere. It was luxury at its finest.

Two servers were assigned to our table. A candle had been lit and the champagne delivered. It was served upon our arrival.

"To a wonderful night," we toasted.

Our glasses touched.

"I love you," he whispered.

May it never end, I thought, taking a long, cool sip from my glass.

James drank his champagne and leaned back, smiling.

In the glowing wick of the flickering candle, I was reminded of how handsome he is, his salt and pepper hair, his intense green eyes and his haunting smile. Despite his well-developed muscles and his good looks, however, there was an innocence about him.

My heart danced like the bubbles in my glass.

We relished in the glow of the champagne as we reflected on our 60 years of friendship.

"Where did the years go?" I asked. "It seems like only yesterday that we celebrated my 16th birthday and here we are celebrating my 76th."

"I remember that day well," reminisced James. "It was also a celebration of a milestone birthday. I'll never forget your reaction when you opened my gift to you." He smiled.

"Oh yes, that beautiful compact! I remember promising to cherish it forever, and I have. It's never far from my heart."

It was only a simple, gold plated souvenir, the type of gift a 16 year old boy would give his special girl, but it was one of the countless small things that connected us, and always would.

Our food arrived. The presentation was out of this world. Even Gordon Ramsay, who once managed the Hotel du Vin kitchen, would have approved.

Throughout the meal our servers were attentive but unobtrusive. They were quick to replenish our water glasses, wine glasses, the bread basket and the butter dish.

Few words were exchanged while we ate. Occasionally, however, an expression of sheer delight broke the silence.

"Delicious," I said of the rack of lamb.

"I agree," nodded James. "It just melts in your mouth."

When we had finished our food and the dishes had been cleared, we sipped and we talked.

What an evening, I thought. I shook my head with amazement. I'm sure it was still whirling when our server returned several minutes later.

"Specialty coffee, perhaps, or cappuccino?" he asked. "Tonight's dessert special is profiteroles, a choux pastry filled with ice cream, topped with chocolate sauce."

"Please give us a minute or two to look over the dessert menu," answered James. "What would you like, dear?" he asked.

"I would like something light. I enjoyed my meal so much that I don't want to spoil it by eating a rich dessert," I answered.

We perused the menu and many choices were tempting, but in the end we both selected a dish of vanilla and strawberry ice cream with an Italian liqueur to round out our meal.

Every spoonful of dessert was more delicious than either of us dreamed.

"A wonderful choice, dear," I said, leaning back in my chair and basking in the golden glow of the night.

The server approached the table.

"Is this a special occasion?" he asked.

"Yes," James answered. "It's Margaret's birthday."

Moments later the server presented me with a unique memento to mark my milestone birthday. It was a white china plate on which the chef had scrolled 'Happy Birthday' in chocolate icing. Delicious Belgian chocolates served as flowers in a colourful bouquet he had created around the scroll.

Breathtaking, I thought.

I was at a loss for words.

Finally, I blurted out, "Thank you so much! What a lovely gesture. This is certainly a birthday to remember."

When we had sipped the last of our liqueur and eaten our last chocolate, the server announced that our taxi had been called and had arrived.

We left the Hotel du Vin feeling that our visit was more of an experience than just somewhere to eat. It was perfect in every way.

The first drops of rain hit the windshield as we pulled away from the curb.

Gentle raindrops were falling by the time we reached the garden. James took my hand and ushered me to the front door.

Suddenly, I turned, smiled and gently placed a fingertip of my left hand on his cheek.

"I love you," I said and it was then that we both realized that I would never tire of saying it.

That night, there was love in the air.

It was the perfect ending to a perfect day.

Margaret Pascuzzo left Scotland in the late 50s and settled in the interior of British Columbia. She always wanted to write for children and that dream was realized in 2004 when she retired from the local school district. To date she has self-published twelve books, three of which have been recognized in Canada and the U.S. A write-up of her entire collection can be seen at margaretpascuzzo.com

FRIDAY RITUAL
By Janet Caplan

Pizza is an ordinary enough food. Oh, you can dress it up or dress it down. Red sauce or white. Pepperoni or prosciutto, Bocconcini, goat cheese or a standard mozzarella: a thick chewy crust or a thin crispy one? Tastes vary, food styles change and the need to refresh a long-standing favorite is hard for some chefs to resist. Whether it's a basic cheese, mushroom and sun-dried tomato pizza or one topped with a more sophisticated gourmet selection, it's still the meal that can satisfy my Friday evening supper craving.

Pizza on Friday night goes back a long way with me and my husband: actually, it goes back to before Donny was my husband and that's quite a long time. We met in university and often we'd go out with friends for that very meal at the end of a long week of studying and playing Hearts. In those days, no one whom we knew had heard of prosciutto or Bocconcini, so our standard toppings consisted of mushrooms, green pepper and pepperoni. And what about a choice of crust? No, I don't think so ... thickish and white floured would be an apt description of what was available. Nevertheless, it was delicious and, in fact, still is.

After university and once we were married, we'd either pick up or go out for pizza to our local pizza restaurant or pizzeria as it was known. I did not enjoy cooking on Fridays after a week at work and although Chinese food was an occasional option, pizza generally won hands down. Besides, our local place knew how to make a terrific pizza and so our ritual continued.

In truth, our consumption of pizza was not solely limited to Friday evenings. Montreal had some fabulous Italian restaurants with menus that included a better class of pizza than our Friday fare. Now that I think of it, maybe Bocconcini did have a home in Canada way back then. Once in a while we'd venture into one of these ristorantes for a special Saturday evening and based on what I recall tasting on those occasions, I'd say that we were definitely eating something above and beyond your average mozzarella.

A few years and a major move later, we found ourselves living in Hamilton, Ontario. We generally enjoyed our four years there but one of my fondest memories of the city is of our Friday night suppers at Italia Restaurant, downtown on John Street. I guess that we may have simply stumbled upon it. We didn't know anyone when we first arrived who might have mentioned it. I'll go with the idea that we may have just gotten lucky when we walked in the first time. I do remember standing outside on the steps leading up to Italia and having the delicious food aromas waft down as people came and went. That was enough to draw us inside.

Italia looked just like you'd expect of a small family restaurant. It was dark with low hanging, brass chandeliers that shed insufficient light yet failed to create the romantic atmosphere that perhaps the owners were going for. The tables were dressed in red and white checkered cloths. Empty straw covered Chianti bottles sat with their dripping candles on each table, alongside a single fresh flower in a vase and the ever-present ashtray ... long ago times indeed. When you sat down in any one of the old wooden chairs, it tilted back and forth: either the legs or the tile floor itself was off kilter.

I know what we ordered on that first visit because I'm almost certain that in four years of Friday evenings, our request never wavered. It was that standard pizza that I mentioned ... mushrooms, green pepper and pepperoni. I liked extra sauce on the side and double mushrooms. Donny loved additional peppers and would eat most of the pepperoni. We always enjoyed a glass or two of Chianti with it.

We'd spend a couple of hours at Italia, leisurely enjoying our food and drink, talking about the week just past, the upcoming weekend and whatever else was going on in our lives: a summing up of events I guess. At the time, the restaurant employed a violinist who would saunter around the small room serenading the clientele. He really wasn't very good, but it seemed like a nice touch.

After a few Friday night visits, we found ourselves being greeted on our arrival by the same young man, as I recall, one of the sons of the owner. This slight, soft-spoken man met us with a smile and a very prompt glass of wine. We were two of his regulars now and he'd always seat us at our particular table at the front, by the window. After allowing us to settle in for a few minutes, he would return, confirm our usual order and be off to the kitchen. The smells emanating through the open doors whet our appetites.

The ritual was a very comfortable one ... very familiar and welcoming. The food was excellent, although I don't recall that we ever got past the pizza, and the service was just fine. Rarely did a Friday night find us anywhere else over that four-year period. Now and then we' be joined at Italia by new Hamilton friends. They all loved the restaurant and did return on their own they informed us, but I think that Donny and I were Italia's biggest fans.

When we did leave Hamilton and move on to Toronto, we looked for a similar restaurant to take its place. We found a very good one, but it never quite measured up to the taste memories that we shared of Italia.

Here I am some decades later thinking about habits and rituals and the comfort they bring. The sameness of the restaurant and the welcome received from a genial host who remembered and expected us week after week were pleasant surprises in an unfamiliar city. More important is our pizza ritual – one that started in Montreal, one that led us to open the door to that welcoming restaurant in Hamilton and one that continues to this day.

For me and for Donny too, pizza on Friday night signals a time to relax and forget about whatever the week was about. Now we generally have take-out from a pretty decent place. Our lives are no longer city lives and rural living means planning ahead. Donny now brings our pizza home. The aroma settles in the car for several hours afterwards and fills the house as soon as he walks in.

Our regular orders have varied over time. Right now, we both prefer thin crust and I stick to double mushrooms and extra sauce with sun dried tomatoes if they're available: pretty basic. Donny, always more adventurous than me, goes out on a limb and selects green olives, fire roasted tomatoes and mushrooms: basic plus.

Our pizzas' spicy, saucy scent and doughy smell have an instant affect on me. They carry me back to the days when pizza Fridays started so many years ago and while I'm reminded of my youth I'm also reminded of the comfort of all the Friday evenings that we've spent together … comfortable with our own personal ritual.

Janet Caplan is a Canadian writer living near Victoria on Vancouver Island. In addition to the variety of anthologies that include some of her personal essays and slice-of-life pieces, she is currently working her way into fiction via a collection of linked short stories set in her fabulous part of the world. Janet's writing about her life, her beautiful natural surroundings and her cocker spaniels has also appeared in several magazines, journals and online.

JUST LIKE IN THE MOVIES
By Lois Kiely

    The inspiration for our elegant dinner for two came from a foreign film playing in New York's Greenwich Village. Damon and I were just 17 and in the throes of first love. We prided ourselves on being young bohemians, cool and artsy. While most kids our age spent Saturdays in the school auditorium cheering for the home team, we haunted art galleries and museums. Our friends teased us for being weird, and our families worried because we appeared odd. We didn't care. In "The Village" the quirkier you were, the better. It was a place that welcomed outsiders, there we were normal.

    For less than a dollar's fare on the subway, we were transported to a venue of free-thinking hipsters and heady intellectuals. Independent movies and off-Broadway plays gave us a taste of cultures beyond our middle class neighborhoods. Damon and I huddled in smoky coffee houses soaking up the ambience and chatting with artists and writers. The Café Wha became a favorite place to hang out. The waiters always dressed in black and didn't mind us sitting for hours at the funky bistro tables. Their unwritten rule was that we had to order something and leave a good tip. We were happy to comply. We got to know one of the regulars pretty well. He was a sculptor named Max.

    Max enjoyed his role as our guide to the Greenwich Village counterculture. When he recommended something to do, we jumped on it. Thanks to his lead, we headed to a little art house that was featuring the latest British flick. I can't remember its title, but the film paved the way for our haute cuisine adventure. One memorable scene featured a well-turned out gentleman and his chic female companion sitting at opposite ends of a banquet table. He wore a tuxedo and she was dressed in a sparkly silk gown that clung to her like a second skin. An officious butler brought out each course in a silver serving dish. He uncovered the domed delicacies with a flourish and awaited the diners' permission to serve. When they gave him the nod of approval, he gingerly placed the food on their plates.

    As they dined they carried on a conversation that was witty and smart. They were the most cultured couple we had ever seen. We fell in love with them. We wanted to be like them, the beautiful people on the silver screen.

    In the darkened theater Damon whispered, "Let's have a dinner like that."

    I thought it would be exciting but I was more practical. "It's out of our league," I responded.

He took my words as a challenge and began to hatch a plan. I knew that somehow he would make it happen.

A few days later Damon called me with a hint of danger in his voice. I could predict that he was conjuring up something that was out of the ordinary. He said that his parents were planning a getaway weekend to celebrate their anniversary. Trina and Angel, his two younger sisters, would be spending Friday and Saturday nights across town with their aunt. He had to stay home to clock in hours at his part-time job.

"We'll have the whole place to ourselves," he exclaimed. "We can have our special dinner right here!" I was skeptical; we didn't know how to cook.

It was late in the afternoon when I arrived at Damon's house. His parents had left for their trip that morning. I rang the bell and Damon opened the door smiling like a Cheshire cat. With feigned formality he said, "Good evening, Mademoiselle" and escorted me to the dining room. The table was set with his mother's fine china, sterling silver flatware, linen napkins, and white taper candles. A delicate Lenox vase in the middle of the table held a bouquet of freshly picked daisies. He remembered that I loved daisies.

"Won't you get in trouble for using her good things?" I asked.

"Not unless you're planning to break something," he answered. His blue-green eyes sparkled with the mischief that I found so appealing. Damon was known as a risk taker. I could be a worrier, but he had confidence for both of us. That coupled with his handsome Mediterranean looks stole my heart.

As I examined the table, my eyes stopped on the crystal wine glasses at each place setting. We were under the legal drinking age and my strict mother would kill me if she sniffed a hint of alcohol on my breath. When he saw the distressed look on my face he laughed and then reassured me by saying, "We're only having ginger ale. But why not drink it from a Waterford flute?"

I agreed with relief and promised not to drop anything.

But there was one important thing missing. "What about food?" I asked.

He said, "I've taken care of it, the Jade Chinese restaurant will be delivering our feast."

I thought that he was probably spending most of his summer job money to pay the bill, but I didn't voice an objection. This was turning out to be too much fun to spoil the moment. Suddenly the doorbell rang and startled me. An impromptu visit from a neighbor would ruin everything. Fortunately it was only the restaurant's delivery man.

Damon had ordered six containers of my favorite Chinese food: won ton soup, moo goo gai pan, shrimp fried rice, sweet and sour pork, vegetable chow mein, and a paper bag filled with fortune cookies. They would be our dessert and I knew we'd read the predictions aloud with stuffy, upper crust English accents. We liked changing our voices to mimic aristocrats.

Before the feast began, Damon left the room and reappeared wearing his father's dinner jacket. I giggled because it didn't quite fit and it was a poor match to his jeans. He walked toward me and slipped his mother's white sequined shawl over my shoulders. Jokingly he apologized for not being able to hire a butler. He said, "We'll simply have to serve ourselves."

We generously piled the food on our plates and took our seats at opposite ends of the table, just the way the sophisticated couple did in the movie. Damon raised his glass of ginger ale and made a toast. "Here's to living well, now and always!" and then we dove into the food.

It has been decades since that remarkable meal. I have a plethora of beautiful memories documenting the years that Damon and I spent together. Like many other couples who fell in love in their teens, we drifted apart in college. But we remained good friends, in fact, best friends.

One evening my husband and I made plans to meet Damon and his wife at a very exclusive restaurant in the city. It was rumored that Jackie Kennedy had called it her favorite spot to dine. The service was impeccable and the food was expertly prepared by a five star chef. The prices were astronomical. When we raised our glasses for a champagne toast Damon said, "Here's to living well, now and always!"

He winked at me and I was reminded that he made the same toast many years ago when we were teenagers who dined like movie stars at our perfect dinner for two.

Lois Kiely is a writer and artist who lives in New Jersey and winters in Arizona. Her story, "My Father's Voice" appears in the latest edition of Chicken Soup for the Soul for Military Families. The Phoenix Writers' Club awarded her first place in their recent 55-word short story contest. Lois is a retired Monmouth University professor, staff developer, and curriculum specialist.

JUST DESSERTS
By Mary Langer Thompson

Now they call it the Paleo or Caveman Diet. Then it was the plain old Atkins Diet. That Friday night at the new barbecue place on Ventura Boulevard near our San Fernando Valley, California home, we ate ribs and steak and broccoli and salad, a meal containing as few carbohydrates as possible. Oh, and a glass of white wine. For the resveratrol. We were full, yet that nagging desire for something sweet to top off our meal lingered. But we were being good and refused the dessert menu.

"I'd really love a red velvet whoopee pie," I confessed to my husband, Dave.

"You'd blow our whole diet? You've lost five pounds. I've lost ten. We just need a little something."

"I can have three lemon drops," I said. "Or how about we each get one of those tiny containers of breath mints?"

"You know I like bubble gum," Dave reminded me. "We can each get a pack."

"Let's go to the Dollar Store and get some," I suggested.

"I don't have any cash. I can't charge that little bit of an amount."

"I'm tired. Forget it."

"No. We'll stop at our ATM up the street. I need money for tomorrow anyway."

As we left the restaurant, Dave nearly tripped over the newspaper stand.

"You need to be more observant," I said. "You could have killed yourself."

*****

It was dark already. We'd turned our clocks back the previous weekend. Dave left me sitting in the idling car on the side street off Ventura Boulevard. I watched while he walked up the ramp to make his transaction at the lit ATM machine.

I always bring a book and thought of turning on the reading light, but I was tired and full. Now I was longing for a piece of that bubble gum. But I'd have to be careful. I didn't want to pull out any fillings. The gum would wind up being expensive if I incurred a dental bill.

I sat and mulled over the current state of dental insurance and then glanced out the window. It had been a long, hard week teaching my high school students. I'd take tonight and tomorrow off and then grade those essays all day Sunday while Dave was at the computer swap meet.

I glanced toward Dave who was still at the machine. A tall, shadowy figure was standing behind him. I could see their backs. I saw Dave nod his head.

Oh brother, I thought. *Dave is such a gabber. What's taking so long? Is the ATM on the fritz? How can he talk so much to a total stranger? One of these days he's going to befriend someone who doesn't feel like talking.*

A few minutes passed. *This is ridiculous. Maybe I should open my window and call to him to please hurry. I want to get home, get in my pajamas, watch TV, and chew my gum. Maybe even blow some bubbles. . .*

Finally, Dave headed toward the car. That other guy was still close behind him. He walked in front of our car, and then took off running.

Feeling irritated, which usually happens on an empty, not full stomach, I opened my mouth as soon as Dave opened his door.

"Do you have to be so darn talkative? Good grief. I want to get home. He could've been a robber."

"He *was* a robber," Dave said between clenched teeth, slamming the door as he got back in the driver's seat.

"You're kidding."

"I'm not kidding." Dave sped off in the same direction as the robber.

"What are you doing?"

"I'm going to get him."

"He could have a gun!"

"He *does* have a gun, and the barrel was stuck right at my temple," said Dave, growing more impatient. He was driving too fast.

"There he is!"

Dave stepped harder on the gas.

I shrank down in my seat. "If he's got a gun, then he could shoot us!" I tend to state the obvious when scared.

But Dave was on a mission. It was too dark to tell whether the guy still had a weapon in his hand, but he was running fast.

The man turned right and ran under an arch leading to a motel parking lot. Dave followed, still determined to be a vigilante.

"You're going to trap him. Then he will shoot us. Turn around." I was pleading.

He whipped into a parking spot, slammed on the brakes, and opened his door. The robber was nowhere in sight.

"What are you doing?"

"I'm going to call the cops from the office," he said.

"Well, I'm not staying in the car this time," I said and hopped out and ran, bent over with my hands over my head.

TABLE FOR TWO

*****

"I just got robbed at gunpoint up the street," Dave informed the manager. The guy ran into your courtyard. Can I use your phone? My cell's at home."

I never carry mine when I'm with Dave. It dawned on me if the guy had shot us, we'd have had to drag ourselves somewhere for help. We could right now be shot and bleeding.

*****

"Yeah, we've been robbed about three times," said the manager, casually handing Dave the phone.

Oh, great. Maybe robbed by the same guy who's going to come in here a fourth time and finish us all off.

I sat down while Dave paced, waiting for the police. He acted like he was on a sugar high rather than carbohydrate deprived.

The policeman greeted the motel manager as though he knew him well. Then he asked Dave to tell him exactly what happened.

"I took out my ATM card," Dave said, "and suddenly I felt something sticking in my back. The guy said, 'Take out $400.00.' I said, 'The limit's $300.00.' He said, 'No, they raised it.' And sure enough, the machine gave me $400.00. Then he said, 'Walk back to your car. Don't do anything funny.'"

I gasped. "Oh, my God, he could have gotten in the car and taken us somewhere and shot us and buried us in a ditch."

Dave stared at me. The manager sorted papers. Was the policeman smirking?

He invited Dave to drive around with him. Dave disappeared fast. I was left in the motel office. The manager made me a pot of coffee, while it dawned on me that if I'd had coffee and their richest dessert at the restaurant, we could have gone straight home.

I really needed something sweet. I dumped five packets of sugar into my coffee.

Soon Dave and the cop returned. Dave looked defeated. The policeman gave us forms to fill out. "You're victims. If you need counseling, you're entitled." He looked at me. "The cameras aren't working at that ATM."

*****

At the convenience store, we charged our bubble gum, but also sour balls, gummy bears, chocolate kisses, for the resveratrol, and a red velvet whoopee pie. Forget that Paleo or Atkins diet or whatever they call it now. We're civilized, not primitive beings.

"How about a movie?" Dave asked.

I chose *Crazy, Stupid Love* because yes, I still love Dave. Even if he isn't always observant and almost got us killed.

Besides, we'll always share a love of sweets.

Mary Langer Thompson is a poet and writer from the High Desert of California. She has been in several anthologies and journals, including Finding Mr. Right *and* Just a Little More Time. *A former principal and secondary English teacher, she is currently the Director of the Dorothy C. Blakely Memoir Project that matches high school students with over-50 "Memoir Stars" to write their stories and to go on to college as published writers.*

BUCKET LIST BISTRO
By Lorelei Kay

Such a long flight! Two flights, actually. First one nine hours from LAX to Iceland, a short layover, and then another three hours to our destination. Hours that would have been spent sleeping if we were back home in California. We haven't slept much. In fact I haven't slept at all. Something about sitting up in a stiff airplane seat instead of lying flat down in a soft bed that precludes any kind of sleep.

But after all the hours of sleep deprivation, our WOW Airbus A321 jet is making its final descent. Beneath our seats I can feel the *bump bump rumble* of the plane's wheels dropping to greet the runway. Not just any runway, but the runway at Charles De Gaulle Airport, the largest international airport in France. And only fifteen miles from Paris. Paris!

Paris, because I'd always dreamed of seeing Paris. The sidewalk cafés, the cathedrals, the museums. Surely even the stars shine brighter over a city like Paris, referred to as "the most beautiful city in the world." And Paris, even more importantly, because we're on our honeymoon. Two 70-year old seniors going for our bucket list. Making a new start together and taking on the world. We're ready to experience all kinds of things, especially all things French—the people, the customs, and the food.

After departing our plane and inhaling a deep breath of European air, the huge airport looms before us. We don't speak French, have no English-speaking tour guide to assist, and can't spot an information booth. Foreign takes on a whole new meaning.

First we must locate the metro station. We're in Terminal 2, which we find is divided into four halls, A, B, C, and D. But they're not in order. After walking a loop and a half through and around the terminal for over an hour, we figure out that the Metro station isn't even in this terminal, but in Terminal 3 instead. We trudge onward, driven forward by the two parallel needs of sleep and food.

After finally locating a ticket booth, we procure our tickets, grab our suitcases, and climb aboard the next Metro to Paris. This kind of ride is another first. Although lots of people get on and off at the many stops, the majority are energetic young guys of various racial backgrounds brandishing colorful tattoos, flamboyant clothing, and wild hairdos. The boisterous energy of their conversations floods the air around us, their energy in sharp contrast to ours.

Thankfully, directly across the aisle from us sits a middle-aged Frenchman with graying hair who looks like a cousin to Richard Gere. A friendly Richard Gere. And he speaks English! We ask him how far our stop *Dupleix* is, and he offers a valuable lesson in Metro taking: the lit green line running above the seats indicates where we are and which way we're heading. It blinks as we approach each station. He points out the window at the frequent stops and shows us how the station names are prominently posted in giant letters so we can keep track of our progress. After 45 minutes he approaches his stop. Before departing, he again points on the map where we need to get off, *Denfert Rochereau*, to make our transfer.

Our first French friend may or may not be a movie star, but he certainly is an angel.

After successfully arriving at *Dupleix*, I pull out my paper giving the directions to locate the Capital Eiffel Hotel. This info came straight from a valid source—a Facebook friend who recommended the hotel. "It's easy," he had explained. "Once you exit the Metro, turn left. Then it's straight ahead."

We start out, dragging our luggage behind us. It's approaching midnight Paris time, although to our bodies it's really 9 o'clock in the morning. Except a pitch black 9 o'clock in the morning. After three blocks and with our hotel nowhere in sight, we suspect we have a problem. We begin retracing our path from the Metro stop, passing a small Bistro where tables and customers spill out into the night. As we step closer, I see the crowd is mostly young folks passing their Saturday night drinking and laughing. I also recognize that it's the Bistro my Facebook friend raved about.

I approach the nearest table and interrupt the partyers by asking directions. I'm met with blank stares. No one speaks English. I try "Capital Eiffel Hotel?" thinking that might translate. More blank stares. We must look like typical lost tourists. Hungry, sleepy, lost tourists. And beginning to feel like homeless lost tourists, dragging all our earthly belongings behind us.

In desperation, we enter another hotel where the gracious concierge Googles the hotel we're trying to find. Success. Hooray! And it's only a half block away. (Note to Self: Don't trust everything you read on Facebook.) We're finally able to we check in and leave our feeling of homelessness behind. A bed. And sleep.

Because of the proximity to the Eiffel Tower, we spend part of the next afternoon exploring the grounds and taking selfies with the towering steel structure as our backdrop. Later we decide to celebrate our first Parisian dinner in the picturesque-Facebook-recommended Bistro we caught sight of the night before. We enter under its red canopy hand in hand, weaving our way past the counter and through tables of laughing couples. Although our waiter speaks no English, it's no problem as the menus offer English subtitles.

TABLE FOR TWO

My handsome husband orders his traditional fare—a hamburger—which is his first choice at home or abroad. I'm more of a broiled chicken fan, but see limited chicken selections. Then I spot it. Salmon burgers! I used to order incredible salmon burgers in the Red Robin back in California.

I enthusiastically point out my choice.

As we wait for our meals, we absorb the Parisian noises and sounds, take in the smell of food on the grill, and appreciate the rise and fall of lilting voices in an unfamiliar language. My honey's burger comes first, and it's looking good. As I wait for mine, I replay in my mind how long I've dreamed of coming to Paris and how thrilling it feels to sit here in a Paris bistro for dinner.

As our waiter places the porcelain plate in front of me, I eagerly scan the food. The bun looks a bit skimpy for a city that celebrates its bread, but that disappointment is quickly overtaken as I look at the piece of salmon. It's salmon, all right. Bright pink salmon. Wait, it is possible? Yes, I think it is—this thick chunk of pink salmon is *raw*. Not just rare, mind you, but never-saw-the-heat-of-any-type-of-broiler-or-pan raw. My stomach, already a bit queasy from the long flight that upended our days, lurches at the sight.

My shocked eyes fly to our very French, very polite, waiter. "Raw!" I say, my voice trying not to sound like the dreaded tourist I'm determined not to be. "It's raw!"

Although he doesn't speak, his universal body language indicates, "Yes, of course it's raw. This is a problem?"

I can only insist, "But it's raw! I need it cooked!"

Apparently understanding, he scurries away with my uncooked fare. Long moments later he returns with the same plate and same underwhelming bun. This time it's graced with clumps of gray-brown salmon bits. The cooking process not only totally depinked the flesh, but must have done so in a vegetable chopper. And it's now slathered in a sauce so oily it could grease the elevator gears on the Eiffel Tower.

There's no choice but to taste it. I feign bravery. But first I must scrape off the sauce which I do at first tentatively, then more aggressively. I also drag the bits of torn-apart fish along the plate in an attempt to rid it of its stick-it-to-me sauce. With little success. I next turn my attention to the salad, but discover its greenery lies beneath a layer of the same goopy . . . oily . . . white . . . stuff. I keep scraping, but it clings just as tenaciously to the lettuce. We give up and leave the food to its scrape-it-in-the-trash fate.

The next morning we wander along the Seine, take a tour bus of the city, and marvel at the incredible pastry shops where customer after customer purchase baguettes and carry them out in open-ended paper bags.

When it's time to make another dinner choice, we're not daunted. After all, we're in Paris—land of Julia Child! And today's another day. When we both spot a cozy Italian restaurant at the same time, we figure we'll give it a try.

Our hostess, a perky brunette in a red sweater, bounces ahead of us to our table. This time it's not a table for two, but a long table comprised of smaller ones pushed together, which could seat 12. Six times better!

We both order a tried-and-true-old-favorite, spaghetti and meatballs. And when it arrives on large steaming platters, neither of us have ever smelled something quite so out-of-this-world deliciously decadent. It propels spaghetti sauce to a whole new level of yum. Everything and more my Paris fantasy had promised.

As we leisurely share our sumptuous meal, I suspect that even after returning home, whenever I think of my favorite dining experience in Paris, I'll think—*Italian!*

Lorelei Kay is a mom, a grandmother, and a writer. Ever since her dad sat her down and helped her write her first poem, she was hooked. She recently published her award-winning memoir, From Mormon to Mermaid. Her poems have appeared in anthologies and magazines. Lorelei has served on the Blue Ribbon Judging Panel for Scholastic Arts and Writing Awards, and also as a mentor and editor on the Dorothy C. Blakely Memoir Project.

TEA FOR TWO
By Kate Guilford

The cell phone's ring jolts me.

"Hello?"

"Hey there, what're ya up to?" Relief threads through my body as I hear Robin's sexy voice with hints of her Texas roots.

"I'm sitting in a stall in the women's bathroom at the Dushanbe Tea House trying to get myself together."

"Oh, honey, are you all right? What happened?"

"No, I'm not," I confess. "I'm so anxious that I'm about to jump out of my skin."

"What's going on, darlin?"

"I'm here for my first date with a man from Match.com, and I just don't know if I can do this." There, I'd said it out loud.

"Good for you for going on Match. Have you emailed with him much?" she cooed.

"Only a little. I just went on Match a week ago today, and right away he wanted to get together for dinner. I put him off for a while and then countered with tea. Now here I am stuck in this bathroom stall on the verge of hyperventilating."

Aromas of exotic spices waft through from the nearby kitchen causing my stomach to gurgle. I look around at the grey metal walls of my protective chamber. What am I doing here? I'm 60 years old, haven't dated since I was 42, and never since Rheumatoid Arthritis wreaked havoc with my body.

"So, what part is making you so anxious, honey?" Robin's soothing voice continued.

"I didn't tell him about the RA, and I have no idea how he'll react when he sees my hands. I guess I'll just put them on the table right away and see what happens. I just hate seeing someone's face when they notice my hands for the first time. Maybe I just won't look."

In her very best 'this is my girlfriend and you'd better not mess with her' mode Robin says, "You are a beautiful, wonderful, amazing woman, and if he can't see that, he's not worth your time anyway. Besides, he's probably nervous, too. Everybody is at these initial meetings. You'll be fine. It's only tea."

"Yes. Thank God, I don't have to try to choke down food while meeting with him. I'd probably gag and end up with stuff streaming out of my nose. I'm not meeting with another guy until I've known him longer and have told him that I have RA. It's too stressful for someone to find out this way."

"Good idea, honey. Now are ya ready to go out there and meet this dude?"

"I guess it's time."

Still edgy, I navigate the busy dining room scanning for someone resembling the small picture on my computer. I approach the hostess. "I'm meeting a man that I don't know. Are you aware of anyone waiting for someone?"

With a knowing look she replies," I don't think he has arrived yet. You're welcome to wait here"—gesturing to a cushioned bench by the door—"or at the bar."

"Thanks," I mumble as I plop onto the bench and pick up a *Boulder Weekly* trying to look engaged rather than nervous. I look through the pictures and headlines, all the focus I can muster. I finish the Weekly and begin to peruse the *Colorado Daily*. Now I'm annoyed. After pushing so hard to meet, is it asking too much for him to be on time? My phone indicates that he's 15 minutes late. If he's not here in five, I'm leaving.

"Hi, Kate," says a tall man I don't recognize. "Let's get a table."

We follow the hostess and settle in by a window. Sitting across from him, my mind races. He looks so different than his picture, at least 10 years older. Looks like he cut himself shaving this morning. Is that shirt the best he could do when he's meeting someone for the first time? I'm annoyed and grumpy that he kept me waiting. I force my attention to the menu. He orders lunch and tea. Then asks what I want to eat. I should have seen this coming when he insisted on the 12:30 meet time.

"I'm not hungry," I lie. I only agreed to tea.

He says, "It's lunch time. You may as well eat."

I ignore him and ask the waiter, "Are these the only decaffeinated teas that you have?"

"Yes, but we have many herbal teas on this other page. They have no caffeine whereas the decaf teas have a small amount."

"Thanks. I can do a little caffeine, but herbal's probably better today." I order a tea that's supposed to balance your chakras, figuring that I can use all the help I can get right now.

"Why can't you have caffeine?" he asks when the waiter leaves.

"It rattles my nervous system and makes it hard for me to sleep."

"It's early. It won't hurt you," he says with attitude.

Instead of giving in to the urge to fight or flee I tell myself to give him more of a chance. I know I can leap too fast sometimes. I attempt to mask my annoyance and make an inane comment about the chakra tea.

Picking up on this, he says, "I went to the Deepak Chopra program yesterday in Westminster, and they talked a lot about chakras."

"Did you find it interesting?"

"Somewhat. All this stuff is new to me. I went to learn more about a product my son wants to sell. I'm helping him start his business. You must know all about chakras having been a massage therapist."

"Some." I know I'm being evasive but can't seem to help it.

Animatedly he instructs, "Show me the location of all the chakras."

I feel immediate rebellion in the face of his authoritarian manner. "No. I'm not here for a test," I say with a smile.

"Sure, you are."

With measured patience I say, "No, I'm not." No smile this time, and I hate that shirt.

Just in the nick of time the food and tea arrive. Thank goodness, a distraction. My relief is short-lived when I realize, as my tea steeps in its pot, that at some point I'll have to pour it with my not so capable hands. Arghgh! Why couldn't it just come in a mug? Maybe he'll offer to pour it for me. Maybe he'll go to the bathroom, and I can pour it while he's gone. "Beam me up, Scottie."

"Your tea is steeped now." He offers no assistance.

The dreaded moment has come. I figure out an awkward way to manage the teapot with my crooked fingers. It looks weird but is stable and safe. I don't have to worry about not looking at his face because this pouring is taking all my focus. I really don't want to drop the teapot. We both act as if nothing unusual is happening. I'm thinking, "Does he see my hands? Is he too shocked to speak? Is this his way of being polite? Is he planning his escape?"

Instead of addressing the obvious issue, I ask when his wife died. "Ten years ago."

"Do you miss her?"

"I was married for 35 years and 30 of them were hell. No. I don't miss her." Then he launches into a litany of complaints about all the women he has dated from the Internet over the last six years. Now I hate that shirt more than any I've ever seen.

As he drones on, I soothe myself by looking just past his left ear at the colorful handmade ceramic tiles. The intricate patterns are mesmerizing. I listen to the water splashing over stones in the central fountain area that includes lush green plants and seven hammered copper statues of women. It's a lovely space and helps takes a bit of the edge off. Suddenly I'm on an exotic adventure in old Tajikistan before the ravages of war. My handsome, attentive companion will return momentarily saving me from this death by boredom.

As my attention is dragged back from afar, the conversation degenerates even further into one about traffic tickets which goes on way too long. Just as I'm thinking that I've got to get out of here, he abruptly throws some cash on the table and stands up saying, "I don't want to get a parking ticket."

To avoid the embarrassment of being left sitting alone, I scramble to stand and walk out with him. Outside he asks, "Do you ski?" It's the only time he's showed any curiosity about who I am. Is he blind? Did he see my hands? They aren't exactly user friendly for ski poles.

"No, not anymore." We shake hands briefly and hurry off to the haven of our respective cars.

I quickly get in, lean back, take a deep breath and say out loud, "At least that's over, and I survived. I'll never have a first Internet date again. It's got to get easier from here, right?"

Kate Guilford followed a colorful patchwork quilt of careers through much of her adulthood, settling into Hakomi Therapy in 1993. Surrounded by the natural beauty of Boulder, Colorado she also enjoys writing Creative Nonfiction, facilitating Life Stories workshops and leading Creative Aging classes. She loves movies, reading and time with friends. She encourages freedom, connection and creativity for everyone.

THE LAST TIME I SAW PERRIS
By Nina Ramos

If I were eight or ten years younger, I would have been over the moon with excitement about my first date with David.

"You two would look so cute together!" my best friend said. Sandy was the one who had introduced us to each other at a Christmas party. Six weeks later, he got up the nerve to ask her if I was seeing anybody. I don't always trust Sandy's judgment when it comes to set-ups because she primarily focuses on the physical. I like a nice-looking guy as much as the next person but it's also important to me that he has a job, that he's well educated, that he doesn't live with his mother, that he doesn't do drugs, and that he doesn't have more baggage than a luggage carousel at O'Hare. Not only did David meet all these requirements on my check-list, he was also into mountain-biking and tennis, liked sushi, spoke three languages, and knew his way around a kitchen.

And then Sandy told me that David was 28.

"He looks older," I said.

"And you look way younger," she replied. "Split the difference and you can both be 32."

I don't know why I've always had such a hang-up about a guy being younger than I am. I did, however, break up with a high school boyfriend because there was a four-*month* age difference. I'm sure it would never have come up in a conversation but, nonetheless, I knew it would rattle around in my brain forever.

When she told me David was eight years younger, why did I immediately feel like a cougar? Would I really be so vain as to turn down a first date with a guy I'd been so attracted to and who had made me laugh at a party?

I asked Sandy if she thought I should break it to him right from the outset. "Why don't you just see if you have a *second* date?" she recommended.

I wondered if enough clues would accidentally slip out over the course of dinner that he'd either do the math himself or not really care.

A rule of mine on a first date is to take separate cars. That way, if things really go south, I have an exit strategy. I also have the strategy that Sandy calls me on my cell about an hour into the date. If it's going badly, I answer and fake an emergency that will require me to leave. If it's going great, I let Sandy go to voice mail and then prepare myself to be peppered with questions the next time I see her.

He arrived ahead of me and was waiting at a table that offered a see-and-be-seen vantage of the whole room. He gallantly stood up (he gets points for that!), kissed me on the cheek (more points!) and pulled out my chair. Was it possible he was even better looking than I remembered from last December?

After complimenting me on my appearance (which I secretly confess to having spent three hours on), he asked if I'd like to start with some champagne.

"What are we celebrating?" I ask. A Friday or Saturday maybe might merit bubbly but this was only Tuesday.

"Let's celebrate that it's Tuesday," he says without missing a beat.

The female server who takes the order asks us if it's a special occasion.

"Tuesday," David replies.

"That is so sweet!" she exclaims. "I wish *my* boyfriend did stuff like that."

Our date isn't even five minutes old yet and someone already thinks we're a couple. David is smiling (I swear he has Robert Redford dimples!) and so he obviously doesn't mind.

He asks how long I've known Sandy.

Is this a trick question? Does he know how old Sandy is?

I serve up a vague reply of, "It feels like eons!"

"Good friends are like that," he remarks.

We order appetizers and start talking about our respective jobs. He's a wealth management consultant. I'm a hairdresser. For reasons that escape me, he finds my job fascinating. Or maybe—dare I hope?—he finds *me* fascinating?

We're in the middle of laughing over a story I'm telling him about a colorist I used to work with who'd steal from tubes of *our* color at the end of the month when she didn't have enough money to buy her own. "Not a whole tube," I explain, "but she'd squirt out just enough product that we weren't supposed to notice any was missing." The problem, I go on, is that hair color is a lot like alchemy and you have to mix things in the right proportion. "Her poor clients never got the same color twice because it depended on what she'd been able to pinch when we weren't looking. She'd tell them that she thought it would be fun to 'go a different way' and then rave how stunning they looked."

David laughs. "Who knew so much intrigue went on behind the scenes in a salon?"

It was at that moment, I realize someone seated across the room has gotten up and is walking straight toward us. That *walk*. What is it about the sassy hip-sway way she moves that looks so familiar even though the woman walking it isn't at all familiar to me? She has a mane of jet black hair, a prominent widow's peak, artfully applied makeup, a form-fitting jersey dress with an alarming reveal of cleavage, and a pair of stilettos that add a good five inches to her height.

"Nina ...?" she ventures, flashing a smile so bright white it could only have been induced by chemicals. "Is it really *you*?"

I give her a quizzical look. "Yes ... uh...?"

"Oh Gollysocks!" she squeals. "How *long* has it been, girlfriend?!" She leans over to do the air-kiss thing.

On the one hand, it's long enough for me not to have made the connection that this is someone I supposedly know. On the other hand, I've only known one person my whole life who says 'Gollysocks'. And has The Walk. Except the last time I saw him, his name was Perris and he looked like Hank Azaria playing Agidor in *The Birdcage*.

Well, this is awkward. What does one say in this situation?

"You look ... great," I say. Not entirely original but a nice feint.

"I *do*, don't I?" she agrees with me. Her glance falls on David. "And who's *this* hunkamus maximus?" she wants to know.

As he extends his hand and introduces himself, she follows suit. I notice that her fingers are sporting thick, inch-long acrylics in black and white. Not a look for everyone but 'she' has managed to make it work. "Yvette Duquesne," she says, "but all my besties call be Evie." She gives me a wink (those false eyelashes are enormous!) and indicates David. "Not too shabby, girlfriend."

Her glance falls on the champagne and she wants to know what we're celebrating.

"Tuesday," we reply in unison.

David asks her how long she's known me. I, in the meantime, just want to sink through the floorboards.

She laughs. "Nina and I go way, *way* back," she replies. She asks if I'm still at the same salon and wants to know who-all of the old gang is still around.

On the heels of my reply, she tells us both that she got out of the 'curl-up-and-dye' biz a few years back and is doing professional modeling now. "We should do lunch and catch up," she tells me.

She glances over her shoulder and remarks that she really needs to get back to her friends.

Another air-kiss.

David is smiling at me over the rim of his champagne flute. "That was interesting," he says. "I take it you hadn't seen her in a while?"

"Oh, you don't know the half of it ..."

We're still talking about it halfway through dinner. David wonders, and rightly so, whether Perris just likes to dress up as a woman and underneath is, well, still Perris.

"I don't think so," I reply. I fuzzily remembered a story he'd told me once on a slow day at the salon about how he had always loved dressing up in his sister's clothes. Maybe even back then he had wanted to be something other than who he was. As an adult, maybe he had saved up enough money to finally become his authentic self. I remember how he said his ultra-conservative family disowned him when he came out as gay and they didn't want any further contact with him.

Becoming Evie would *really* have made their heads explode.

I recall lots of little things about Perris I had forgotten. The way he liked to sing along (badly) whenever a George Michael song came on the radio. The way he'd weep genuine tears whenever a client remembered his birthday and brought him flowers. The way he'd decorate his station mirror with a riot of feathers. I remember how all of us loved that Perris could crack us up with hilarious stories. From the way his companions across the restaurant are laughing and smiling as s/he holds court, it's clear that Perris still has a fine tuned sense of audience. Strange a reconnection as this has been, I truly hope he—or, rather, she—is happy.

"At least your friend can finally be truthful," David comments.

Ouch. I'm reminded that there's still something hanging in the air between us. I really like David. I know I really want to see him again. And I also know that sooner or later the age thing is going to come up and he's going to wonder how many *other* things I haven't told him about myself.

"Speaking of honesty …" I begin.

"Yeah?"

"There's … uh … something I need to tell you."

A worried look descends on his handsome face. "What is it?"

I take a deep breath and reveal that I'm 36.

He lets this sink in, briefly, before issuing an exaggerated, "Whew!"

Whew? Not *exactly* the reaction I was expecting. "'Whew'?" I echo.

He closes his hand over mine and says, "I was almost dreading you were going to tell me that your real name used to be Norman."

First-time writer Nina Ramos is now co-owner of the same salon where she first began her hairdressing career after graduating from beauty college. She is also happy to share that she and her hubby, David, just celebrated their fifth wedding anniversary—an occasion which, she notes, fell on a Tuesday this year. Champagne was involved.

SOULFUL BONDING
By Sarah Stein

    We sat in silence for a moment as I watched the reflection of the four-course meal. The three-lit candle caused it to dance along the gold-plated vase centerpiece. The braised chicken sat elegantly against two loaded baked potatoes, and steamed broccoli situated between the vase and candles. Breathing near the wick would cause the fire to move creating a separate shadow elsewhere in the showpiece. I was in a trance for a moment until Dustin snapped me out of my reverie by his slight movement.
    He gradually picked up the silver fork that was wrapped inside of a gold-trimmed napkin before stabbing into his bowl filled with green lettuce leaves, chopped tomatoes, and covered with a blend of American and Swiss shredded cheese. His moan of approval drew a smile from my lips as I watched in awe.
    My core tightened by that slight action. Dustin's tongue darted out before grazing it softly along his upper, and then lower lip. That act alone made my blood boil. I wasn't sure how long I could sit through this meal without ravishing more than just the food. Out of the 16 years we had been together, not once had I thought eating under candlelight could be this unsettling.
    With each bite, I wanted so badly to lean over the small, distressed table, and lick the remaining remnants from his mouth. Yet, I stayed rooted to my seat and lifted the stem of my wine glass that was filled with the sweetest Moscato, the perfect liquid for this occasion.
    No one was around. We were alone in our two-story home, while the kids chose to spend the night with their friends. It was peaceful and quiet, which was something that's hard to get, but very much appreciated.
    Who would've thought that observing my spouse chew his meal could be such a turn-on? Dressed in black slacks and a tailored button-up lavender shirt with long sleeves that were rolled up to reveal his tight muscles, he was a gorgeous specimen, and one I was proud to call my husband.
    His mouth remained closed as his jaw continued moving, devouring the bits of food. I yearned to lean over, and run my fingers through his shoulder-length brown hair, but fought against the feeling.
    Once again, Dustin had snapped me out of my daydream, "Baby, this meal beat any that you've ever cooked in the past, and that's saying a lot."
    I grinned at his comment, and from the wink that had followed. It's true. Throughout the years, I've been a terrible cook, only following recipes, and

never quite getting the flavor right. This time though, I wanted our meal to be perfect. Why? Well, today marked a huge milestone for us. We had just hit fifteen years of married.

To most people, that's not a huge deal, but to us being together this long meant many more years to follow. We had gotten hitched at a very young age, and were told by numerous friends and family that we wouldn't last. Well, as I gazed toward my husband, I silently thanked whomever above that we were fortunate to care and love one another enough to make it this far.

I grasped the tongs before placing a slice of chicken onto each of our plates while replying, "You haven't eaten the rest. So don't compliment my cooking just yet."

We both chuckled at my response, but he knew that I worked hard to make this night memorable. Dustin reached his right hand across the table and grasped mine before squeezing tight. That tiny bit of assurance pleased me because he understood precisely what to do, or say in any situation that would arise.

After releasing my grip, Dustin sliced into his own piece of chicken before chewing it. He moaned once again, and I knew exactly what he had tasted, the succulent meat burst with flavors as it touched our taste buds.

As soon as Dustin swallowed, he revealed, "I take that back. You're such a terrible cook."

His face was so serious when he spoke, but I knew better. Dustin was full of jokes and picked on me every chance he got, so I leaned across the table this time with the intent to swipe at his arm. Instead of making contact with the arm, Dustin clutched my hand between both his palms. His reflex was quick.

"Don't start what you can't finish," he warned through a burst of laughter.

His head tilted back as his Adam's apple moved with each bellow. Damn, that man made me clench my thighs with want. After all these years, how could such an act make me all hot and bothered?

We stayed that way for a moment knowing full well we should finish our meal. Dustin tightened his hold before he slowly let go of my hand displaying a gorgeous smile that lit up his eyes. I was mesmerized by every little detail, motionless under the sheer intensity of his gaze. By staring into the depths of his eyes, we connected on a whole other level.

Dustin leaned back before taking a small sip of his drink and then grabbed a few more bites of the meat and potato. All the while, he held my gaze. His hazel eyes read me like a book and seemed to know precisely what was on my mind, if the smirk of his was any indication. Our attraction hadn't diminished one bit after all these years, and I didn't expect it to now. But was it possible that it could be stronger?

Finishing off the final bits of food on his plate, Dustin murmured, "So, how about dessert?"

"You know me. I never forget the best part of the meal," I batted my lashes and then giggled.

Heat pooled once again, but I wasn't fooled, and neither was he. If I knew Dustin at all, he meant the fun kind, not edible. But I played stupid and smiled while I uncovered the extra dish on the edge of the table. It was a slice of dark chocolate mousse cake, and one I had to buy from the restaurant down our street. I knew better than to try my luck at baking, since I sucked at cooking in general.

Either way, Dustin didn't care one iota if I spend little time laboring over a meal, as long as there was something edible in the kitchen. It didn't have to be prepared by me. As soon as the cover came off, he slid the fork into the cake breaking off a bite-sized portion.

I went to grab my own piece, but saw his cake-filled fork blocking my path. There weren't many times when Dustin fed me because I tended to steal bites while he wasn't looking. This time, however, I opened my mouth wide enough to receive the piece before enclosing my lips around the utensil. Out of all our sensual moments, this one probably topped them all. He slowly pulled the fork, but I didn't release it right away because I lapped up every bit of chocolate that coated it.

Dustin's eyes widened in surprise, and I knew by his sudden shifting on the chair that he was just as bothered. We both wanted more and knew it, but I wasn't done yet. Retrieving my own dollop, this time much larger, I repeated the gesture of inserting it into his mouth. Instead of closing his lips, his tongue cradled the bottom of the utensil before using his top teeth to remove the morsel, closing his eyelids as if savoring the rich flavor.

After two more bites of the sweet chocolate, Dustin announced, "That was delicious. And not just the cake, but I'm not fully done with dessert."

My head jerked up as my eyes looked his way. The grin plastered on his face almost had me choking. I knew that look, the one where he wanted to taste me next. He tossed the napkin on the table before heading to the fridge. I sat still wondering what Dustin was doing, but I didn't have to wait long. When he walked back to where I rested, I noticed the can of whipped cream just as he urged me to get up.

"Let's finish what was started," he growled in my ear, causing butterflies to take flight.

"But what about the dishes?" I questioned as he enveloped my fingers in his.

"To hell with them. They're not going anywhere but you, my dear, will fly to the Heaven's above after I'm done with you."

Many years together, and he still caused tingles along my skin forcing goosebumps to the surface. Dustin didn't have to comment further, because I'd follow him to the ends of the Earth, past the universe, and into other dimensions, if it were remotely possible. And just like that, he continued to hold the key to my heart.

Sarah Stein has always been an avid reader. Her love for books at an early age is why she started creating her own stories. Today, she's a multi-published author with works in various genres. She's from southern Louisiana but resides in South Texas with her husband of many years, and two children. When she isn't spending quality time with them, she's singing, reading, writing, or researching for her latest work in progress.

LUNCH IS INCLUDED
By Raghavendra Rao

My wife Usha, and I are on a short visit to the States from India. Our six-year-old granddaughter, Shanthi, is with us.

Ramesh, my son, calls me early in the morning from Los Angeles and suggests, "Dad, since you are in San Diego, take a half-day tour to Tijuana. There is a museum and an arts center. Shanthi will enjoy the Botanical Gardens."

"Let's go to Tijuana," says Usha putting stress on the letter "J."

At the lobby of Howard Johnson Inn, a travel agent, Rafael, sits at a table displaying his nameplate and colorful brochures, oozing hospitality. We introduce ourselves.

"Mr. Rao and Mrs. Rao, what tours interest you? Sea World? Zoo? Tijuana?"

"Tijuana. We were at Sea World yesterday," I say.

"Half a day tour or a full day? How about the 'lunch is included' option?"

The agent looks at me. I look at Usha.

"Let's have lunch there. I want to taste authentic Mexican food," Usha says.

"Please note, we're Brahmins, strict vegetarians," I say.

"Don't worry, Mr. Rao, You'll be dining at the La Casa Restaurante. Excellent place. They have plenty of veggie choices."

"It's a big city, I heard. There must be many vegetarians in Tijuana. Moreover, it's a tourist center." Usha comments, facing the agent.

"Yes, yes, you're right." Rafael nods his head, collects his fee and hands us the travel and lunch vouchers.

The next morning. Usha wears her favorite green sari and a pink blouse with a flowery border. She looks like a beautiful rose bud among green leaves. Shanthi is in her *ghagra choli*. We are at the lobby early.

"Let's have breakfast here at the restaurant," Usha suggests.

"Usha, this will kill our appetite and we won't be able to do justice to our lunch."

"I'm hungry." Shanthi whines.

I buy a sandwich and a glass of milk for her. She starts to eat and spills bread crumbs on the sofa.

The tour bus arrives on time. The driver gets down and invites us. "From India?" He queries with a smile.

I nod.

"Colorful dress. Your wife's beautiful."

Usha blushes. She is not used for such comments in India.

The bus stops at a shopping area in Tijuana. Hawkers loudly beckon us to step into their shops. "Senorita, ten dollar purse, only five dollars for you," they shout. Usha bargains and gets a leather one with intricate designs for four dollars. Shanthi has a pinwheel. We all don sombreros and sit on a cart pulled by a donkey with painted stripes. Shanthi feels ecstatic and is convinced it is a zebra. After a couple of hours, the bus driver takes us to a downtown area and parks in front of La Casa Restaurante.

"Mr. Rao, lunch is preordered for your family, enjoy," the driver says. Then he and fellow travelers melt into the crowded street like ice in soda pop.

We enter the restaurant. It is dimly lit, a loud pop music is on and the smell of fried onions, cilantro and chili peppers engulf us. I see a burly customer eating lunch at one corner. Otherwise, the place is empty.

"Senor, Senorita." The server, colorfully robed, wearing a sombrero, greets and shows us to a table, hospitality gushing out like leaking water from a fire hydrant. Shanthi looks in awe at his huge hat.

"*Agua*? Coke? Tequilas, Blanco, Reposado?" the server asks.

I'm confused. Probably he is talking of alcoholic drinks.

"No alcohol. Only Coke," I tell him two times. "It's included in the lunch," I assure Usha.

"Grandpa, I want chocolate ice cream," Shanthi says.

The server comes back in ten minutes, dexterously carrying two platters of food with metal lid covers,
Coke and a large bowl of ice cream. He places them on the table in front of us with a red Hibiscus flower for decoration.

"*Disfrutar*," he curtly says, bows and walks away.

Usha is hungry and removes the lid in a hurry. The smell of sizzling steak and sautéed onions hits our nostrils.

"Oh, no, we don't eat this." She covers her mouth and nose with her sari pallu and slams down the lid.

"No meat, no meat," I say loudly raising my hand.

The server is taken aback and returns to our table. "*Problema?*"

The burly Hispanic gentleman eating lunch at the far end of the hall shouts, "Ramon, no *carne*." The man is obviously a regular customer and knows the server.

The server apologizes, "*Lo siento mucho, señor, lo siento mucho.*"

It's my fault too. I should have told him that we are vegetarians.

"No chicken, no eggs, either," I say.

TABLE FOR TWO

The Good Samaritan helps. "Ramon, No *pollo*, no *huevos, por favor.*"

The server disappears into the kitchen.

Shanthi is happy because she has Coke and ice cream. At home she is not allowed soft drinks. She eats the ice cream slowly so that it will last longer. She plays with the straw, blowing bubbles into the Coke, making funny noises. She fishes out a small chunk of ice and balances it on the fork laughing. "See, Grandpa," she says. The ice slips down and slides under the table.

Now I see three Hispanic men wearing huge sombreros and colorful clothes entering the restaurant. One carries a violin, the other a huge guitar and the third one has a drum. Smiling benevolently, they surround us and start singing. I don't understand, but this is royal treatment. Shanthi gets up and dances.

The song is over and I think they'll leave us in peace. No. They start another one. Soon this song is finished. Then they start a third one. The violinist bows close to my wife and passionately breathes part of the song and cigar stink over her face. It is probably a love tune.

Usha is annoyed.

The husky man at the corner tells me, "*Señor*, tip the singers, give dollars."

I place five dollars on the table. They stop singing and the violinist picks up the money.

"*Gracias, gracias,*" he says and respectfully bows. They move to a corner of the hall, sit and order three tequilas. Peace at last.

With a smile exuding confidence, the server comes back with plates of food and puts them on our table.

"*Camarón, Señor.* No *carne*, no *huevos*, no *Puerco*," he announces.

The Good Samaritan is ready. "*Señor*, they are shrimp. No meat, no eggs, no pork. Enjoy."

I can see these shrimp and their long whiskers. I am speechless.

Usha studies her plate. "Oh no, those eyes are staring at me," she shouts.

The server rises his hands up and murmurs, "*O, Dios, como les puedo ayudar?*"

Just then the bus driver enters.

"Mr. Rao, what's going on? The server is frustrated and wondering how he can help you."

"We are vegetarians and I'm unable to convey that message. He is serving all kinds of non-veggie dishes."

"I'm sorry. Come, we have to go back. A few passengers have to catch planes in Los Angeles."

"We haven't eaten anything yet."

"Sorry. We must leave now."

We get up. Shanthi is reluctant to leave her ice cream. "Grandma, can I take it with me?"

"No, you'll mess up the seat."

"*Señor, dólares para la Coke,*" the server reminds us. He thinks we will give him the slip. Obviously Coke is not included in the lunch deal. I place ten dollars that covers the tip as well on the table and we leave.

When entering the bus, the driver stops our granddaughter. "What's your name, cutie?"

"Shanthi. I'm in kindergarten."

"Thank you. Already in kinder? Proud of you. Wait."

He opens an ice box and picks up three packets wrapped in brown paper. "Santi, these are cheese sandwiches. Hundred percent vegetarian. My daughter packs a few of them daily for me. Here is one for you and these two are for your grandparents."

Shanti's face lights up.

The driver faces us, smiles and says, "On this tour, lunch is included."

Dr. Raghavendra Rao is a pediatrician practicing in Porterville, California. He has published two books on children's health. He is a health columnist to a local newspaper, the Porterville Recorder and has contributed about 200 health articles to the paper. His fiction short stories, about 30 of them so far, have been published in Siliconeer, a Bay area magazine. He is married and has two children, who are both doctors.

TABLE FOR ONE
By L. J. Hecht

Call me old-fashioned but when you take someone out to a nice dinner, is it too much to expect them to give you their undivided attention?

I'm showing my age, I think, when I see young people on a date night and they can't stop checking their cellular phones or sending text messages. It's not just half the couple doing it, either; they're both so absorbed in communicating with other people that the person straight across from them could choke and need a Heimlich and they wouldn't even notice.

The first Sunday after my wife and I got back from our honeymoon, we went to a neighborhood pancake place and I took along the newspaper. "Why did you bring the paper?" she asked. I told her that I thought we could pass the sections back and forth while we were eating. All the years I was a bachelor and went out for breakfast before work, I didn't think twice about this habit. From my new wife's perspective, though, it meant that less than two weeks after we said our vows, I must have thought the newspaper was more interesting than she was. And so I never did it again.

I also draw the line when it comes to flirting with the opposite sex. No man wants to compliment a pretty female server in front of his wife without the risk of her asking if he thinks she's younger and prettier. There is, however, a double standard when wives giggle over the attention paid to them by buff and blonde waiters young enough to be their grandsons. I believe I have lived this long for not pointing out the age discrepancy to her.

My wife isn't given to obsessions but on the occasion of our 40th anniversary, I saw a side of her I hadn't seen before. I'd made reservations for a Saturday night dinner at a fancy restaurant. Fewer and fewer of our friends these days have made it to that matrimonial milestone and I was feeling rather proud. A lot of the spouses we know in their 70s have succumbed to illness or, in the case of a few husbands in the throes of a randy midlife crisis, have traded their older wives for a newer and curvier model.

I complimented my wife on the dress she was wearing. She also went to her hairdresser and manicurist that morning and I remembered to compliment her on this, too. I put on my best suit and gave her an orchid to pin to her dress. It would be an evening to remember!

We began with cocktails. Two sips into hers, my wife suddenly started staring at an attractive woman who was being seated a few tables away.

"Someone you know?" I asked.

She shook her head and continued staring.

Maybe she thought the woman was a movie star, even though we don't live anywhere like Hollywood where celebrity sightings would be commonplace. Certainly she wasn't anyone *I* recognized but I put it down to not watching much television or going to the movies. Again, I'm showing my age but I prefer watching old movies on Turner Classics because the women *and* men were not only good looking, they could also act and convince you of the roles they were playing.

"I wonder who she's waiting for," I heard my wife remark.

"Probably her husband," I replied. I asked her if she'd like to start with an appetizer but she seemed more transfixed on watching the woman.

A few minutes later, my wife observed that the waiter was taking away the second place setting, all the while smiling and laughing with the woman as if they were old friends.

"Now he's bringing her a glass of wine," she said. There seemed to me to be a bit of censure in her voice.

I tried to bring her into a discussion of what she thought we should order.

"Do you think she's been stood up?"

"Why would you think that?"

"Because she's obviously going ahead and starting without him." She tells me again that the second place setting has been removed.

"Do you think she'll order an entire meal?"

She indicated that the woman was thoughtfully looking over the menu.

"Well, it *is* a restaurant," I reply. "Maybe she'll go really bold and order dessert, too."

My wife rolled her eyes in annoyance that I was being obtuse. "If she was hungry, why couldn't she get something to go?" For that matter, she added, why couldn't she have stayed home and cooked?

"Maybe she doesn't know how," I offered.

"Well no *wonder* she doesn't have a man in her life! What man wants to marry a woman that can't cook?"

"*You* didn't know how to cook when we got married … and here we are decades later."

My wife retorted that it's all right if a girl is young and just learning her way around a kitchen. "But *that* one—she must be at least late 40s."

"Yes. What a relic."

"You're not taking this seriously. I mean she's attractive enough but what kind of woman brazenly eats alone in an expensive restaurant?"

I pointed out that I really didn't think it was a crime. "Maybe she's on a business trip," I suggested.

"On a Saturday night?" Saturday night are date nights and family nights, she informed me. Clearly this attractive woman didn't have either one.

"Maybe she's a widow."

"She's not wearing black."

"Maybe she's divorced."

"Then why isn't she having dinner with a girlfriend to cheer her up?"

"Maybe she doesn't need cheering."

During this exchange, we both noticed that two other waiters stopped by her table to chat and she had a beautiful smile for both of them.

A few bites into our appetizer, my wife made a different observation. "You don't suppose she's a—"

"A what?"

"You know." She lowered her voice. "A *working* girl."

I know my wife well enough to understand she wasn't referring to a female executive who works in one of the downtown high-rises. "Where do you come up with these ideas?" I asked her.

She shrugged and continued watching, intent on missing nary a clue about this woman's vocation and why she was dining alone.

I was briefly reminded of a turn-of-the-century song (I sang barbershop quartet after I got out of the Navy) called "She Is More To Be Pitied Than Censured." The only lyric I remembered after all these years was something to the effect that a man had been the cause of the poor creature's downfall. Except that this attractive woman dining by herself didn't fit that category. Had I mentioned this to my wife, it would only add more fuel to her need to cast aspersions on a complete stranger.

The chef came out briefly to greet her with a big smile and kiss her hand.

"She obviously knows the people who work here," my wife said.

"Maybe she's the owner."

She quickly dismissed that speculation. "If she's the owner, why isn't she eating in the kitchen?"

"Maybe she wants to observe how workaday folk like us are enjoying the cuisine."

"But she hasn't looked our way once."

Yes, for that I was grateful.

"You'd never catch *me* doing something like that," my wife confided.

"Something like what?"

"Eating dinner alone in a fancy restaurant on a Saturday night. She doesn't even seem to *care* what people are thinking."

"The mark of a supremely confident woman," I murmured, quietly envying a stranger enjoying a nice meal in peace.

"What?"

"Nothing," I replied. "How's your lamb chop?"

L. J. Hecht is a retired botanist whose only writing prior to this was a series of field guides used in universities. He and his wife are coming up on their golden anniversary. His only remembrance of the Table For One woman is that she looked like Grace Kelly and had trim ankles—neither of which he has ever mentioned in the interests of staying alive.

OUR CANADIAN SUNSET
By Terri Elders

By the time Ken and I flew to northeast Washington State to shop around for our future retirement home, I'd lived, worked, or traveled in exactly 49 countries. But I'd never set foot in Canada. A native Californian, I'd always envisioned our neighbor to the north as a kind of frozen wasteland dotted with icebergs and igloos. And now my husband of not too many years wanted to move to a county right next door, edging the Canadian border.

He'd explored the area solo a summer or two earlier, on the recommendation of his son who often had visited Stevens County to fish on the Columbia River or to play golf. And he'd liked what he'd seen.

"The Colville National Forest actually is high desert," he'd explained, urging me to at least give the place a try. "Let's consider it seriously. There's four seasons, a fifth if you count Indian Summer. And I'd never let you freeze to death. I promise."

Still, I'd read that temperatures plunged below zero in the winter, so that January I'd taken a week's leave from my Peace Corps job in Washington, DC. I suggested we reconnoiter the area in the dead of winter before we committed to such Ken's proposed move. I wanted to see if indeed I could survive in sub-zero temperatures without turning into a life-size icicle.

During that initial first brief visit our realtor escorted us up and down Stevens County's Highway 395 corridor. We tramped through ranch houses, log cabins and even farmhouses, from Loon Lake to Kettle Falls, slogging through snow to reach each entryway. By Saturday, weary and chilled, I felt relief when our realtor announced she took Sundays off.

"Thank heavens. I'll a chance to thaw out."

"We could drive up to Grand Forks in British Columbia for an early Sunday supper," Ken suggested the next morning, peeking out the window. "It's doesn't look like it will snow today and it's less than an hour and a half from here. We'll take our time and really enjoy dining out."

"What a delightful idea! The rental car does have a good heater."

I grabbed my jacket and mittens quicker than anybody could say Jack Frost. In the motel lobby I snatched up a brochure about Canada's Boundary Country. Grand Forks, I explained to Ken as we headed north, had been called the "jewel of the Boundary" and had been settled by Doukhobors. These were Christian pacifists who'd fled the religious persecution of Russia's 19th-century czars. Russian was still taught in public schools.

"The Doukhobors sound as if they had much in common with the Quakers," I added. He grinned and nodded. He knew I'd attended a Friends church as a child.

"You'll probably like them then," he said.

When we finally reached the Canadian checkpoint, I pleaded with the border guard to stamp my passport, even though he claimed it really wasn't necessary. I wanted solid proof that I'd finally arrived at my 50th country. I'd been keeping count for a long time, and planned to brag to my colleagues at Peace Corps headquarters when we returned to the capital.

The landscape we'd traversed on our drive turned out to resemble more closely the Currier and Ives lithographs I remembered from Christmas cards than it did the barren Frozen North of my imagination. When we pulled into Grand Forks, though, the little town appeared shuttered down for the winter. I didn't spy any welcoming lights.

My brochure had informed us that Grand Forks, BC, derived its name from its location at the juncture of the Kettle and Granby Rivers in the area's "Sunshine Valley." Hard to understand why the area earned that nickname. Not a glimmer of sunshine was breaking through the glowering overcast skies that frigid day.

Getting hungry, we pulled up in front of the Grand Forks Hotel, an Edwardian Classical Revival structure that we later learned had survived devastating early 20th Century fires. Its restaurant was closed that Sunday afternoon, but a sign on the door announced that meals were available in the bar.

"Great," Ken said, as we settled at a little table set for two, nicely set with a checkered table cloth and matching linen napkins. "I'm ready for a steak!"

When the waiter appeared, I asked what beer he would recommend. I'd glanced around at the few diners and noticed that they all seemed to be enjoying identical bottles of a golden-hued brew.

"I figured you must be tourists," he said, with a smile. "Everybody here, of course, drinks Kokanee. It's brewed in Creston, a town just down the road a stretch."

He brought a couple of bottles and some glasses to our table. "Look for the Sasquatch on the label," he said, "You can't miss him. His name is Mel."

After we located the Bigfoot icon mascot, we perused the menus. No steaks. Instead, it offered us a selection of borscht, perogies, hamburgers and fries.

"What's a perogy?" Ken asked. "I know that Borscht is beet soup."

"They're potato dumplings. I ate some in Ukraine. They're addictive! I'm going to have some. If we're drinking local, we might as well eat local."

So, we ordered the soup, as well. Neither of us had ever been fond of beets, but we hadn't driven all this way to settle for burgers. The perogies, accompanied by a creamy dill sauce, appeared as crisply inviting as the ones I'd sampled in Ukraine. Our borscht was thick with cabbage, onion, beets, and carrots. We dipped our dumplings into the dill. Umm. Not bad at all. Then we each spooned up some soup. At first taste, we gazed at one another. We'd fallen in love. It was drop-dead delicious, the perfect hearty dish for a gloomy winter day.

As we headed that evening back to our motel, I turned to Ken and grinned.

"Canada's a perfect 50th country for me to add to my list. This has been a golden afternoon."

A year later Ken and I, long since settled into our Stevens County home just south of Colville, discovered that our upcoming fifth anniversary on July 1st was also Canada's national day. Since it fell on a Friday in 2005, I suggested we take a long Independence Day weekend and celebrate Canada Day in Grand Forks and come home to Colville in time for July 4th fireworks.

Ken concurred. "I'm ready for some more borscht!"

This time we sampled the luscious velvety red concoction at The Borscht Bowl, in a heritage bank building in downtown Grand Forks. We spent the afternoon wandering through the festivities in the city park, and visited Mountain View Doukhobor Museum, a collection of artifacts and heirlooms set in one of the last original Doukhobor communal homes. We drove out to the Spencer Hill Orchard and Gallery, admired their contented cows, and picked up some organic Gouda, Ken's favorite cheese, for snacking later at our motel.

We dropped by the local bowling alley, ordered a couple of Kokanees, and watched locals compete at five-pin bowling, a variant played only in Canada. I puzzled over how the bowlers could get a grip on the hand-sized hard rubber balls that lacked any finger holes. Somehow, they never fumbled.

We lingered outside our motel room to watch the sunset together, and then settled in to catch some cable television. Ken delighted in finding a local channel running a marathon of his favorite old western series, "Have Gun, Will Travel." He'd always admired its black-clad gun-for-hire, Paladin, a man of ethics and conscience. In fact, Ken knew all the words to only two songs, "You are My Sunshine," and the theme song from Paladin. He even treated me to a few bars as the show closed. Then he hugged me close.

"What more could I ask for on an anniversary? I've got you, borscht, Gouda, and Paladin. Life's good."

And it continued to be for a few more years. Then Ken died, just three weeks short of our ninth anniversary. On what would have been our 10th, and another Canada Day, I drove up to Grand Forks by myself. Perhaps revisiting my golden 50th country would cheer me.

Doukhobor women, in their head scarves, were selling handicrafts and ice cream in the park. I wandered through some of the art galleries that Ken had loved, and visited a new one in the Palladian-style red brick courthouse. Then I treated myself to a bowl of aromatic borscht at the hotel where we'd first become enamored of borscht. I looked across my table set for two at an empty chair, and silently toasted Ken's memory with a Kokanee, after checking the label to make sure that Mel, the Sasquatch, was still atop his glacier. He was.

Each prior visit when Ken and I left Grand Forks to head south, we'd steal a last lingering look at the nearby Hardy Mountains. We'd pretend to search for Mel in the shadows of the evening sunset.

This time, though, as I scanned the mountains, I fantasized that I could catch a glimpse of Ken. He'd be riding alongside his friend, Paladin. He'd be wearing white in contrast to Paladin's black. The pair would be heading towards a hitching post outside a cozy saloon where they could down a Kokanee and savor a bowl of borscht. Perhaps they'd wave to Mel on their way.

I crossed the border into Washington, reflecting. Ken's absence loomed large in the front seat of our vehicle. Nonetheless, it had been a good, if not grand, 10th anniversary in Grand Forks. I'd be home by sunset, still missing my husband, but aglow with tasty memories.

Terri Elders, LCSW, a lifelong writer and editor, has contributed to over 100 anthologies, including multiple editions of Chicken Soup for the Soul. *She writes feature articles and travel pieces for a wide variety of national and international periodicals. After a quarter-century odyssey, including a decade overseas with Peace Corps, she recently returned to her native California. She blogs at http://atouchoftarragon.blogspot.com/*

ABOUT THE EDITOR

Former actress and theatre director Christina Hamlett is an award winning author whose credits to date include 39 books, 167 stage plays, and squillions of articles and interviews that appear online and in trade publications worldwide. She is also a script consultant for stage and screen as well as a professional ghostwriter.
Learn more at www.authorhamlett.com

If you enjoyed *Table for Two*, might we also recommend:

Made in the USA
Lexington, KY
03 April 2018